PARENTING
PIE

PARENTING PIE

Learn the Secret Ingredients for Teens

Authored by

PRAVEEN SINGH

Penman Books

Office No. 303, Kumar House Building,
D Block, Central Market, Opp PVR Cinema,
Prashant Vihar, Delhi 110085, India
Website: www.penmanbooks.com
Email: publish@penmanbooks.com

First Published by Penman Books 2020
Copyright © Praveen Singh 2020
All Rights Reserved.

Title: Parenting Pie
Price: ₹299 | $11.99
ISBN: 978-93-89024-49-4

Acknowledgement

Writing a book has been an experience, which, is something beyond words. As much as it sounds rewarding, so much difficult, it is to put your thoughts into words. My book-writing has been a dream come true and I cannot thank God enough for it.

Dreams can never come true without the support of loved ones and well-wishers. I am eternally grateful to the following people, without whom, I could have never penned down my book. I know this is going to be a long list. However, I would not like to miss an opportunity to express my love and gratitude to them.

- My husband, *Praveen Kumar*, who has stood by me, taking up my share of responsibilities at home, co-operating in every way possible and encouraging me to live-up to my dream.

- My daughters *Prateeksha* and *Prerana*, who have been those first Teenagers of the current generation in my life, observing whom, I learnt the other side of the story.

- My son ***Advait***, who has been really excited to see his mother becoming an author, and tracked my progress minutely every day.

- My ***Grandparents, In-Laws, Parents, Aunts, Uncles***, watching whom, I grew up from a Teenager to a Parent myself.

- My ***Cousins***, who are my Buddies, and whose love never made me feel I am the only born. They have always looked up to me as a *Role Model* and have made me more responsible to *Take Charge*.

Apart from my family, there have been a few eminent individuals, whose entry into my life has been instrumental in creating the required positive aura around me, which helped me achieve what I dreamt of…

- My mentor ***Arfeen Khan***, my ***backbone***, who not only empowered me to dream big and push myself out of my comfort zone but also showed me a path for achieving my dreams.

- My ***Master Mind*** group of coaches who have always been there for me whenever I need their help; motivating me at every juncture.

Love You All

Preface

Every parent has his or her own style of parenting. With all due respect to every style of parenting, I would like to suggest the parents to drop off their guards and read this book with a fresh perspective. Reading with an open mind would give you a better insight into the concept of Transformational parenting.

Innovation and Adaptation are the key aspects of survival in this world. Therefore we, as parents, should be more flexible in adapting new techniques to befriend our Teens and make them feel more open to engage in a dialogue with us.

Research has found out that the way we parent our children has a lot to do with the way we were parented. In the earlier generations, only repeating the parenting principles or rules was all that was necessary for being a successful parent. In short, we first learn parenting in our childhood by observing our parents. We then implement it when we become parents ourselves. We do what we had observed our parents do. In case we are not lucky enough to remember, we go by what our external influences say – friends, aunts, uncles, colleagues.

But, wait, is this still applicable to the current generation?

Times have changed and so have the requirements of the children. What is learned can also be unlearned and new techniques can be adapted.

"EVERY BOOK NEEDS A NEW EDITION; REPLACING THE OLD ONE, SINCE THE SYLLABUS KEEPS CHANGING."

As the kids grow until their Teenage, our regular parenting principles, which we carry forward from the previous generations, stay applicable and are adhered to by them. The kids listen to us and we feel they are under our control. However, what actually happens is that the child registers and accepts every instruction of ours, as there is no external influence. Later, when they enter their Teens, other influences appear - friends, teachers and social media. Therefore, there is a change in their decision-making. A disconnect is created between what parents say and what the external influences say. Now the children slowly start using their intellect to decide what is it that they actually want to do. Sometimes, this results in the child taking decisions on his/her own, which go against the parents. Therefore, insecurity starts creeping into the parent's mind. They end up saying, *"My Teenager seems to be getting out of my hands (control)."*

This is the stage where the parents feel their child has started disobeying them. Slowly the gap starts surfacing, and a conflict arises.

The Teenager says *"My parents do not understand me."*

Parents say *"The child no more listens to us."*

Both parties will hold their perception right, as they would end up having a justification for their side of the story, irrespective of whether it has been investigated through a litmus test.

In this book, I will reflect on all the attributes that we, as a parent, should consciously consider while parenting our Teenagers. We will first get introduced to what we call 'the problem', as it appears and the attitude-change of our Teenagers. Then we will look at what are the apprehensions that are bothering us so much that our relationships with our Teenagers suddenly get strained. Later, we will try to dive into the Teenagers' world, which we might have never ventured into, so far. Once we understand their world inside-out, we will also be able to appreciate their side of the story.

Progressing further, we will learn about a new perspective of parenting as a recipe. We will master the ropes of why it is thus and how to come up with a yummy PARENT-TEEN recipe that appeals to both you and your Teenager's taste buds.

I have not assigned any chapter numbers in the Index since I think Parenting is more of the quality we brew in as a parent and less of quantity. So, let the numbers not barricade your transformation........

Contents

Acknowledgement   *v*

Preface   *vii*

The Beginning   *xiii*

My Story   1

The Problem   11

New Attitude of Teenagers   15

Parents Apprehensions   21

Teens World Uncovered   27

    Physical Transition   29

    What is with their Brain?   31

    Challenging Conversations   33

    Unruly Behavior   36

    Emotional Fluctuations   37

    Social Implications   38

    Sibling Rivalry   39

    Grandparents   41

    Summary   43

DOs Vs DONTs — 47

  Things To Do List — 49

  Things Not To Do List — 63

Parenting – Visualize it as a Recipe — 71

  Why a Pie ? — 74

  Basic Ingredients of a Parenting Pie for Teenagers — 76

  Ingredients for Crust — 76

  Ingredients for Filling — 90

Add Your Creative Juices — 157

Customized "Parenting Pie" Recipe for Your Teenager — 161

  Ingredients for Crust — 163

  Ingredients for the Filling — 165

  Ingredients for the Toppings — 166

  Method — 168

Summary and Best Wishes — 169

THE BEGINNING

Dear Mom/Dad,

Gone are those days of giggle and wiggle

These are the days of surprises and struggle ...

I am no more a kid; this is what, you ask me to learn

But alas, you always forget, you treat me like one ...

I am going to be an adult; will have to take charge, is what
I believe

Each time I try to become one, I am crossing my limits, is what
you feel ...

Things are changing, in, and around me

Why don't you look at this world, as, how I see ...

I wish to explore, and learn things on my own

But, I get scared, when I fail, and see you frown ...

I want to wade through this phase, going through, trial and
error

But you always want to hold me, in the warmth of your feather ...

You are my strength; I know I can rely on you
It is my new intellect, which says, it is not always true ...

In conflicts at home, you expect me, to be more adjusting
But what to do, I yearn, to make it more challenging ...

I want to fly high, fall down, soar back and learn
Even if I know, my feathers are going to burn ...

I have no control, as the fascinating world attracts me
I want their validation, and am eager to know, what they think
of me ...

Each time, I might have, something different to share
All you want to know, is in exams, how I fare ...

You are like an eagle, watching every move of mine
Please try to understand, I am going to be just fine ...

You have lots to share, since you are perched on a wisdom tree
I wish to learn on my own, and hate those advices for free ...

Don't make me a person, I don't want to become
Every comparison that you do, I struggle to overcome ...

I may be insensitive, to your feelings sometimes
My intention was not to hurt you, many of those times ...

Please teach me values, but give the freedom to think
Do not wet your eyes, every time you blink ...

Deep down my heart, I know you are always there
Whatever the situation may be, you will really care ...

Sometimes I mess up, but please continue watering trust
I might be asking for more, but kindly adjust ...

When you look at me, you try to find yourself
All I want to find in the mirror, is, an identity for myself ...

...Your Teenager

My Story

Yes, I do have a story. A story, which made me realize I have been asleep for the last few years because everything that I had done as a parent until my transformation, seemed to have suddenly vanished. It was time to change my thought process and also of many other parents who were going through a similar phase or entering one. There might have been many authors, but, my thoughts have never been written before, and my story has not been told before.

I am the original aspect of my creativity and what I bring to this world will be different from what others would have brought even on the same parenting topic.

"Everybody is original if he tells the truth if he speaks from himself. But it must be from his true self and not from the self he thinks he should be."

—Brenda Ueland

When I named my daughter "Prerana", I did so for two reasons:

- so that her name rhymes with 2 of her only cousins then, Prateeksha and Ashna,

- a lovely meaning of the name – Inspiration.

Little did I know that one day I would myself get inspired by her to follow my passion!

Many Teenagers like my daughter get either distressed or aggressive if things do not happen the way they want. They get upset very quickly for anything and everything. As a parent, for the past few years, I too reacted bitterly each time I faced this rebellious behavior. As a mother, I wanted to show her, how she needed to behave. What would the world say one day – *"Her Mom did not know how to raise her daughter to be a socially amiable person!"*

I had really got tired of facing these situations. On one side, I was exasperated at this intolerable behavior, but on the other side, I was dreaded of the consequences of the arguments, knowing the volatile and vulnerable nature of a Teenager's brain. Luckily, my Teenager proved my fears wrong. Irrespective of the magnitude of the fight, we had, she never ever uttered any depressive words. She yelled and argued back, which was fine with me. She did not want to face me and so would continue being serious for many hours and sometimes days. However, I was fine with that behavior.

During those serious verbal give-and-take episodes, she sometimes spoke a few things, which made me realize, I also had a few flaws, which I was ignoring myself. I understood she was a strong individual from within. She just reacted to situations, like a kid. Nevertheless, she was growing into a mature young woman. I started realizing that she sometimes behaved like a split personality. She was a darling with everyone around her, except with me. I was inquisitive to know the rootcause behind it.

As any curious mom would, I turned towards our All-time Best Friend – GOOGLE. Sometimes, I wonder what I would have done without it.

It was always there for me whenever I had a question in my mind. I would look up and then add my flavor to the tips it gave. Without a parent's personal touch, there should be nothing that should be applied and I strongly believe in it and hence the concept of a recipe.

By the way, I have two kids. I know I am writing a lot about my daughter because as of now, she currently surrounds my entire world and she has reached an age where I can try to understand her behavioral pattern. In addition, the 10th – 12th Standard years are the ones when the kids get the most of their parents' attention. Nevertheless, my son, Advait, true to his name is a unique personality. He surprises me each time he comes up with some logic of his own. Kids sometimes teach you things, which were never told or taught to you. We should just be ready to willingly accept those learnings and put them into practice. I am going to write about him soon.

So, continuing with my quest for understanding the Teenage behavior, I read a lot of information on the Internet, went ahead and attended a seminar on "Parenting Teens", purchased and read books related to NLP (Neuro-Linguistic Programming). For those of you who are hearing this term for the first time, here are a few details: NLP is a way of life, a new, different, positive approach to the way we communicate, and how we interpret the way others communicate with us both verbally and non-verbally. The only way to make effective changes in our life is to engage with this new NLP way and to incorporate it daily into everything we do.

All that helped me to put myself into a Teenager's role and only then I was slowly able to understand what makes them behave the way they do. Every Kid is different and we cannot conclude on a generic behavioral pattern most of the time. However, you will surely be able to understand the basic framework of a Teenager.

Whenever I tried to introduce some new concepts of behavior to my Dare Devil, immediately came back some strong statements.

A few dialogues that touched my heart

"You always say this but never do It"

"Why don't you first do what you are asking me to" (Practice before you Preach)

Little did I realize that this would lead me to get interested in the concept of Coaching. I have always been an ardent fan of the Teaching Profession. My Mom and my aunts are great teachers and are still into this profession. Teaching runs in our blood ;-). If I were not an IT Professional, I would surely have been a Principal running a school as my Mom did. Therefore, the interest in mentoring, motivating and public speaking has always invaded my enthusiasm. This was something that came naturally to me. I never had a stage fear be it while giving dance performances or participating in competitions. I loved being on stage and in the limelight. However, I was never a person who would try out something daring. I always wanted to be in a safe Horizon and that made me give up on all my passions.

So, when I actually started to attend a few sessions on Coaching and started involving myself in the meet-ups with likeminded people, who were looking for similar opportunities to make this world a better place to live, I realized, "THIS IS IT". During the inception of this new-found journey though my daughter did not express her appreciation verbally but I could sense the silent 'Bravo'. This is what mothers are good at; reading their kid's mind. She encouraged me indirectly to continue on this journey by asking me to go and attend the follow-up sessions. I silently continued working on these new activities, along with my regular job routine and then came this Motivational booster from her.

A note, which she left for me:

"Maa…. I feel overwhelmingly happy now that I see you working on something that you actually love and cherish :-)"

The moment I read this, I felt elated for the first time in many years ….

What better acknowledgment and appreciation I could have got…. I understood that whenever my daughter dared me to do something… it has always catalyzed me to do a small changeover within me … didn't know if it was my anger towards her statements or my love for her which was buried deep down in my heart .... Whatever, it was... it has now inspired me to become a Life Transformation Coach and a Speaker.

I started my journey interacting with Teenagers, parents of Teenagers and doing some free speaking sessions in schools. I collected a lot of information by running surveys for parents of the Teenagers. As I had embarked on this beautiful journey of Transformation, what struck me hard was the number of suicides of some of the Intermediate (XII Standard) students in Telangana owing to bad results or failing in their Board exams.

I really pondered over who was to be blamed... 'the Kids', for their fear of failure and immature decision ... the 'Board of Education', for the constant focus on academics and not focusing on life skills ... the 'Society', that created so much of pressure on them that the kids dreaded to face it ....or the 'Parents', who had every chance of saving them, but they had just not built up the confidence level of their children to face failure.

"THERE IS NO FAILURE IN LIFE...
IT IS ONLY A LEARNING"

The night after my entire research was done, the actual truth dawned upon me, I woke up with jitters. My daughter was not a little girl anymore and there was no going back. I lay there in the pool of thoughts as I realized all the things that I did wrong with her as a parent. Parenting was supposed to be a very simple thing and I just complicated it. I felt guilty and unpardonable. I wished if there was a Time Machine to take me back and I could start all over again fresh with all the learnings that I had now acquired.

My mission is to make the parents of Teenagers, who are struggling, understand that, there is still time to improve the relationship with their Teenager. To let them know

- They can in many new ways connect with their Teenager

- They can get the respect they always wanted to get from them

- They can open up that closed communication channel with their silent killer

Above all....

'Become a proud parent of a Young Adult who is going to be equipped with all that is required to face this world on their own'.

For parents who are yet to get into the phase of parenting Teenagers or becoming parents, this book will help them to be more prepared and not commit mistakes. As the saying goes – 'Precautions are better than cure'. It is better to be on the right track from the beginning rather than getting lost and struggling to navigate back to the right track. How we parent the kids in their Pre-Teens determines what we have in store during their Teenage years. So, try to get it right from the beginning.

YOU ARE NOT ALONE

The Problem

Before I embark on this journey with you, let me first acknowledge that there is surely a problem. The earlier we accept, the better for us. Moreover, the bad news is that there are no quick solutions to it. We think that we can protect our Teenagers from all the bad influences of this world, but the answer is a big 'NO'. We cannot protect them from all the dangers that can hit them hard, we cannot help them avoid the emotional turmoil of their adolescent years.

However, by creating an atmosphere where your Teenagers are free to express what they feel, there is a fair chance they will be more receptive to hearing your feelings, more inclined to consider your viewpoint, more adaptive to any restraints that are imposed. Above all, more protected by your values.

I know, what I have conceived, as the concept of parenting, is a new definition. There are already so many innovative terms introduced by our PARENTS. Therefore, here I am, presenting my concept of parenting, as nothing but a recipe. We feel happy when our babies enter this world, learn new things and grow into independent individuals. What strikes us though is when the learnings, practices, and methods that we have been using for long, start to fail suddenly. We fear the fact that despite our best efforts, we seem to be missing the right as a parent over our Teenager. We are scared if they are really going to be those young adults whom we have nurtured to introduce to this new world.

I have gone through this phase myself and according to me, in real life, the practical experience is more important than theoretical knowledge. This book is all about sharing my learnings, the ones acquired through practical experiences, through seminars that I attended, having discussions with parents and Teenagers. Believe me, I have never felt this burdened even when I struggled and managed to get admission in BITS, Pilani for my graduation. Well, then that is the beauty of parenting, you become more responsible and sensitive when you enter a new phase of life called 'Parenting Teens'.

New Attitude of Teenagers

Samantha returns from college, tired, she drops her bag on the sofa in the hall and settles down in her favorite Beanbag. Her mom who is today working from home and has just finished her 2-hour call says - *"Samantha, how many times have I told you to put things in their place."*

Samantha snaps back *"Mom, you always keep telling me and I always keep doing it. What is the point in repeating what I do not want to or do not like to do? I will take the bag to the room when I feel like. Anyways, there are not going to be any visitors coming to our house today. So, why are you getting so furious?"*

"Furious and me...?" Rachel says, *"I have been so accommodative with whatever you do these days, but there seems to be no end to your tantrums. I wonder if you are the same kid who followed all my instructions earlier!"*

"Chill mom, you guys have an issue for every small thing in life." Samantha leaves dragging that bag on the floor and slamming the door of her room behind her.

Tears roll out of Rachel's eyes, as no one is watching her. She wonders if she is watching the same little Sammy (Samantha's pet name), who would rush to her after coming back from school. Sammy would hug her, kiss her and narrate all that had happened at her school. Now, there is hardly any conversation happening between them.

~ ~ ~

This is the attitude of the current generation of Teenagers. During our Teens, we too had been rebels, but silent ones. We tried to do, or did things which we wanted to, but made sure this was not known to our parents and acted very sweet with them. However, the current generation is more open to their feelings and frustrations. They feel they have a right to do what they are doing. This gives a lot of pain to us as we have always been living in a world of expectations.

At some point, every Teenage kid drives the parent crazy over a bad attitude. The expressions on their faces and their actions speak for them - rolling their eyes, a sarcastic smile, the dirty and scary look, shrugging their shoulder, the sarcastic comment, and a big sigh. These are ways to show their resentment.

Some Teens display their self-assertive behavior as a mark of difference and like to show it off wherever they go. Some act sweet and caring for a minute and turn into an angry and arrogant one the next minute.

I had read this in some book or article and loved it - "While each child is unique, you can categorize their mindset into 3 different ways. Recognizing which attitude our Teen exhibits will help us address the behavior in a peaceful manner."

- **Anxiety:** Suddenly, there seem to be more anxious Teenagers than there are anxious parents. Teenagers feel the pressure of parents, peers, society or culture. We will talk about these in detail in the coming chapters.

- **Anger:** If you have a Teen monster at home, ready to pounce on you on every pretext, please do not worry, you have a hell lot of company around.

- **Arrogance:** Oh My! This is the attitude that can turn a parent into a Hulk. Believe me; my blood just boils at this attitude. "Mom you can never understand" is the statement I hated a lot. With this attitude, they treat us like a bunch of dumb creatures on this Earth.

In the chapter **'Teen's world uncovered'**, we will be able to nosedive a little deeper to understand why our Teens carry these attitudes.

Parent's Apprehensions

When our children enter their Teenage years, we feel proud to have brought them up with all the love, care, affection and everything that was required to turn them into great human beings. As we start celebrating early, all hell breaks loose. Our confidence levels suddenly drop after looking at their changed behavior and attitude.

When I began this journey, I felt I was all alone, only I am the helpless, a weak mom who is not able to handle her Teenager. I really did not have any examples around me. With the research and interactions that I had later with parents of similar aged kids in my workshops, I came to know that the world was full of victim parents. Yes… I call ourselves victims, because, that is the mode we, parents of Teenagers, are in - the VICTIM MODE. Many parents had more self-doubt and apprehensions. After hearing them out, I felt I am in a much better situation.

Questions that intrigue us …

- Why do I feel as if I have suddenly become unfamiliar with my Teenager?

- What is exactly going on in my child's mind?

- Why has my Teenager suddenly stopped sharing things with me?

- Why do our children feel that we are imposing our decisions on them?

- Why is my child always moody, angry or aggressive?

- Why can't my child accept and deal with any kind of failure?

- What, if my child, is getting into bad habits or bad companies?

- Why doesn't my child respect and acknowledge the effort that we parents are putting in?

- Why does my child always suffer from anxiety or low self-confidence?

- Why doesn't my child consider me as a friend anymore?

- Why can't my child realize his/her true potential and achieve great results like others?

- Why can't my child be as disciplined and as understanding as our neighbor's child?

- Why doesn't my child like spending time with me anymore?

- Why doesn't my child sit with me, hug me the way he/she did earlier?

These are the exact questions that I brainstorm with the parents in my program, workshop or coaching session. I convert them into more empowering questions that they can try to get answers. If you look at the above victim questions, they fall into the category of self-pity. I believe that the moment we feel helpless, pity ourselves, our actions fall prey to something called self-doubt and a sense of failure seeps into us. Parents, who have lived their lives with so much confidence bringing a new life into this world, suddenly start getting nervous about how things are going to progress further.

Most of the parents either wait or suffer until this phase passes. However, some, unknowingly, get into higher stress levels thus deteriorating their physical and mental wellbeing. This according to me is a slow poison, which acts slowly, but definitely spoils the well-being of the entire family, and sometimes even the younger kids at home. If you are having just one Teenager at home and no kids younger, you are a lucky one. But if there is one or more than one to follow ... May God save you from going through the same turmoil once again.

Parents going through this distress do not share it outside, as it will hurt their ego. They are happier, showing off as a successful parent rather than discussing and taking help. Well, if you belong to this category, then, frankly speaking, you do not have a right to ask the above questions about your Teenager, as you are behaving like one and not opening up to taking help.

THE
HIDDEN
TRUTH

Teen's World Uncovered

Adolescence is a period in our life when the behavior and characteristics of a person are changing. Our child is slowly transitioning into an adult. Changes in the body are the ones most immediately observed. However, there are other subtle characteristics changes that start to appear. The way the kids think, how they behave and how they interact with others slowly keeps changing. The speed with which these changes occur differs from individual to individual.

PHYSICAL TRANSITION

Body changes affect the physical appearance of the individual such as the height, weight, fat and muscle distribution, glandular secretions, and sexual characteristics. We know that physical changes can affect the emotional quotient as well as the thinking process of a person. As the hormone fluctuation occurs, we see the thought process and the display of emotions in the Teenager saddled on a roller-coaster ride. The Teenagers will start having their opinions and will be ready to comment on other's behavior. They feel their parents are unnecessarily worrying too much or trying to get overprotective.

However, a Pre-Teen child will never be able to comprehend something like that. Many physical changes are common to both girls and boys. These range from growing bigger in size to changing preferences for a variety of foods. Their brains are developing fast and they look for constant changes in the way they satisfy their emotions, food cravings, etc.

Many girls start menstruating earlier these days compared to previous generations. Sometimes it is as early as age nine or ten. Gone are the days, when menstruation was considered a taboo. As a parent, and especially if you are a mother, you need to prepare your girl for what is in store for her. The best way to handle this is by asking questions:

"Smita, how much do you know about menstruation?
What do you know about your first period?"

Questions are far better than lectures.

I was shocked when I tried to start a dialogue with my daughter when she was around 11 years. To my surprise, I came to know that she was already aware of it as her teachers had a session the previous year and explained to them the entire thing. She went a step ahead and shared that she was the only one in her class who was yet to have her first period. These days, there are many schools that are taking this initiative of having separate sessions for girls to educate them on menstruation and first period. This gave me a big relief as the Education system is slowly changing and equipping the kids to face 'LIFE'.

The bond between daughter and parents should continue to develop as the daughter develops physically. Usually, fathers tend to keep themselves aloof in all such scenarios, which is fair enough if that is what is required. Nevertheless, kindly note that your little angel who is turning into a beautiful woman may interpret this hesitancy as rejection and start distancing herself from you. Therefore, it is better for fathers to appreciate the fact that their daughters do need that emotional touch irrespective of their age. In addition, if you are a single father, it is more important for you to play the role of both a mother and a father.

When it comes to boys, their hormones kick in a little later than female hormones. Parents should be able to discuss sexuality with their sons just as they do with their daughters. If Mom hesitates doing this, let the Dads initiate the talking. Make sure to use the questioning approach, which according to me is the best to approach for the parents. Question them, let them think and come up with their answers. And do make sure, you ask something called open-ended questions for them to be able to express more.

WHAT IS WITH THEIR BRAIN?

A Teen's brain undergoes tremendous changes in structure and chemistry. The external environment shapes your Teen's brain growth just as in toddlerhood. Current findings confirm that the adolescent brain is indeed changing. For parents who are interested in getting details, you can find huge information easily accessible on the internet and I would really recommend you to quickly browse through some.

Our children are slowly transitioning into their independent thinking styles after they cross 10 years of age. As much as they were inquisitive about the world around them when they were toddlers, they enter the same arena of inquisitiveness, of course now with different intentions. They now would like to question human behavior, why her Mom is that way…why Dad reacts in this manner…why their sibling acts so stupidly. What is hurting though is that they do not do this in a pleasant manner. Most of the time, it is accompanied by anger, resentment, mockery, and retorts.

They suddenly feel they are ready to take charge of their own life and can handle any situation that comes their way. They get confident that their judgments have very strong logic behind whereas the ones of others do not. This slowly gives air to the misunderstanding between the Teen and their parents.

Parents start feeling they are now living with a complete stranger at home. The following are the typical behavioral changes that your Teenager might display:

- They no longer wish to share stories about their school, friends or their daily routine.

- They scan everything that is said to them with their intellectual and logical filters and come up with their own innovative meanings and conclusions.

- They start questioning your values against which you have raised them.

- They do not hesitate to pick up an argument if you are not able to see their point of view.

- They keep switching roles between a Hero and a Villain.

- They are your best buddies at one moment and daredevils in the next one.

I know these things may be really taking a toll on you as a parent and may dip you down to the lowest levels of your confidence levels. However, it is important to understand that these changes are a natural and important part of a child's development. If you feel confident that you have raised your child with good values, relax and chill. This is just a phase, which will pass soon. Your child would be all set to face the world when it is the right time.

CHALLENGING CONVERSATIONS

Teens sometimes are the most difficult ones to converse. Sometimes they say the most outrageous things ever. Therefore, do not judge them soon. The following are the reasons why they do that.

- They want to hear what is right. They want their parents to respond and give them the right perspective, and so they try to provoke the correct information.

- They want interaction and attention. If Teens are expecting for some emotion and reasonable comments do not elicit a response, they will try a different approach. When parents do not express joy and excitement over the right things, Teens will seek negative reaction over the wrong things. An apathetic reaction is as bad as an inflexible reaction.

- They want to make the parent upset and feel pain because the parent-child relationship is not good. When Teens are in pain, they want their parents to recognize it and feel it too. An outrageous comment can give them the momentary satisfaction they are looking for and they get excited over it.

- They use the conversation to get control. Shocking declarations or statements attract parents' attention — though reluctantly. Suddenly, the Teen starts initiating and the parent starts reacting. At that moment, the Teen is in control; the parent is not. This gives the Teen a feeling of power.

- These encounters are evidence of the psychological changes in the adolescent phase. As children turn into Teenagers, their mental wiring is maturing and falling into place.

- Teens are easily able to comprehend these observations, but not in a courteous way. They might make a very justifiable comment on their parents but in a rather unruly manner. Parents fall prey when they try to challenge their Teen's psychological development by reacting back in a harsh manner. It is very important not to shut down the communication channel by talking harshly to them. Instead of reacting, it is better to respond.

In short, Teens' psychological development is what happens when their new mental capability interacts with the old values that we as parents have imposed on them. They want to build up their own value system, by challenging the old ones that they have been carrying forward since their childhood. To cope up with this reality is surely going to bc tough for us as parents.... However, we should understand that this is the reality and not a myth or a rumor. What saves us though is our intention to keep the dialogue going. If a parent is not a good communicator, then it is time to learn the art and become one. Sometimes, it is better to present our thoughts and let them decide rather than dictate them how to think, how to feel or what to do. You remain safe as long as you are on the other side of the battle. The moment you end up threatening them or saying something that hurts them, you have given up and lost the battle. You would never get back a chance to face them or have a dialogue with them.

Not all Teen psychological development issues involve outrageous comments. Some choices in the new values that they are developing are destructive and can threaten a Teen's personality or slow down his or her development for a number of years. If we feel our Teens are going to do something that will mess up their life for a long time to come, it is our responsibility to protect them by taking help and getting a Therapist or a Counsellor involved. Nevertheless, make sure to think twice before taking up this responsibility of getting help. If you are not careful, your fears could override your judgment in making this sort of decision. Whether or not forcing a Teen into a treatment environment is wise often depends on the expertise of the staff at the treatment center.

UNRULY BEHAVIOR

When thinking about this aspect of a Teenager, I would just recommend you to close your eyes for 5 minutes, get back to your Teen years and think of all that you did, to irritate your teachers, your parents and everyone around you. What we need to keep in mind is that during our Teenage, we had been rebels too, but maybe silent ones. All that we did, most of the time, we hid it from our parents. After all this, have we not grown up to be socially amiable beings? So, why do we get offended when our little ones are going through the same phase? The only difference between them and us is, they are more outrageous than what we were. We are supposed to be the more matured ones, are we not?

All the changes that they are going through physically, emotionally and psychologically are making them what I call the "TEEN MONSTERS". They hate to be a replica of their parents and by doing what they want to do; they want to prove themselves more INDIVIDUALISTIC, more INDEPENDENT and SELF MADE. Children raised with a unique identity for themselves, often do not display this rebellious phase as they have a strong belief system about themselves and a high self-esteem.

The Teenagers who went through strict Military discipline and had to follow orders tend to break loose and become more rebellious, as they feel they have suffered long enough. Children having protective parents are not much better off, as their protective shield is going to be broken soon. So, all that you have to do is understand the uniqueness of your child and try to boost up their confidence levels rather than trying to raise an army or hover over them like a drone.

In summary, if you have had a great relationship with your kids from their birth, this phase once passed, everything is going to get back to normal. Even if your child has turned into a Hulk, you can befriend him/her, once they get back to their normal self. However, if not, it is never too late to mend some of our ways.

EMOTIONAL FLUCTUATIONS

Well, it is not done yet… the story continues. You are a lucky parent if your Teen does not attack you with their emotional highs and lows. Be patient and be prepared for the below:

- They show their strong feelings and intense emotions at different times. Their moods might seem so unpredictable and you see a new pattern each time. These emotional ups and downs can lead to a lot of conflicts. Your child's brain is still learning to control and express emotions in a matured way. Sometimes it is successful and sometimes not.

- They start getting more sensitive to parent's emotions. They get better at reading and processing others' emotions. While they are developing these skills, they can sometimes misread facial expressions or body language and react in the wrong way.

- They become more self-conscious, especially about physical appearance and changes occurring in them. Teenage self-esteem is often affected by their appearance - or by how Teenagers think they look. As they develop, Teens might compare their bodies with those of friends and peers.

- They go through an unquestionable stage of thinking and acting as if nothing could go wrong with them. Their decision-making skills are still developing, and they are learning the consequences of their actions through trial and error.

SOCIAL IMPLICATIONS

Teenagers start looking out for their identity as an individual in society. Their gender, their friend circle, family and cultural background, media, their educational institution, family and relative's expectations, could influence this. They might try to seek more independence to make their role stronger in comparison to others.

They also start looking for new experiences and are more prone to risk-taking behavior. They start listening to their friends more than their parents or family. They create some ideologies and make friends with the ones who give importance to them. Their communication shifts from verbal to digital as they consider it the latest trend. They start looking for validations from their peer group personally as well as through social media. Such is the impact of technology advancement.

SIBLING RIVALRY

Sibling Rivalry… at this age? If these questions crop up in your mind, please ask parents who have more than one kid at home, and that one kid I am referring to is our Darling TEEN Monster. The Teenager longs for independence and at the same time does not want the sibling to get more attention from the parents. They make sure, the rules that the parents made the Teen adhere to become a Rulebook for the little one too. After mending our ways of parenting, even if we want to let go in case of the little one, it becomes a challenge for us, as our Teen is standing in front of us, ready to question this relaxation of the rules. This has been my own personal experience and with many other parents.

The typical dialogues are -

"Why do you let him get away with what he wants?"

"I always followed your instructions and excelled, then why don't you make sure she does the same?"

"Why can't you teach him the value of money? Money does not grow on trees."

"How dare she talks to me like that?"

Well, when parents hear these words, all they could recollect was that these were the same dialogues told to the Teenager by either parents or someone from the family, while they grew up. They are trying to repeat the same mistake we did. Observe parents and do what they did. They as the elder sibling, daunt the role of parents now. If you allow them to continue this way, without transforming yourself in front of them, imagine the destruction it would cause when the Teen becomes a parent and repeats the same behavior.

Every kid is different but mostly in the family, the first one turns out to be the Doer... The Engineer, The Doctor... The Lawyer and so on. As we move ahead in our parenting journey with the second or third kid, we get a little relaxed and allow the kid to be what they want. Well, this is something the elder one hates as a Teenager. It could possibly be the other way round. The Teenager might be the younger one and constant comparison with the elder one might result in hatred deep down in their heart.

So, if you have more than one kid at home, please watch out for any symptoms of sibling rivalry. Most of the time, it shows up but sometimes it hits hard like a silent killer and comes out only once the kids grow up and blurt out about it. While all kids are technically equal to the parents, surely underlying favoritism shows up. Try to be more sensitive to the Teenager's requirement. It might not sound appealing if I ask you to spend more time with your Teen compared to the other child or favor them, but please try to be a little sensitive to their feelings. Most of the aggressive behavior they show with their siblings might not be true. We need to identify the actual root cause.

GRANDPARENTS

Having grandparents around for the children is a blessing in disguise for the parents. There are so many things that the grandparents can do which might not be possible for parents. The kids get enough love and affection, especially when both the parents are away for work. Grandparents who stay with the children in the same house or in close proximity are important sources of life lessons. They can convey these lessons to their grandchildren not only through stories but also with general experience and knowledge. Grandparents help children develop strong moral and social values. If any unfortunate incident happens in the child's life like losing a parent in an accident, parents' divorce, parents suffering from any terminal illness or financial difficulties, the grandparents form great moral support to the children.

All this works fine until the kids enter the Teenage years. They slowly start getting isolated from their grandparents as they expect more privacy and more space to adjust to the physical and psychological turmoil going on. If the grandparents are the ones who try to parent them by advising, then the situation gets even worse. This does not happen in every case. A few grandparents do not wear the parent hat and try to wear a friendship hat. They connect to the Teenagers like one among them, take them on a road trip, and get back to nature. During these activities, the Teens tend to open up to them more compared to the parents. However, there are a few grandparents, who can only visualize the things going wrong with the Teens – phone addiction, spending less time with family, bad grades, wrong friendship, not willing to mingle during social gatherings, etc. They can never get over the fact that their grandchild has now become a rebel and their children are not taking measures to curtail this behavior. If this is the situation, it becomes all the more difficult for the parents to handle the Teenagers. They end up becoming cheese in the sandwich. On one side, they upset their parents if not adhering to their value system and on the other side; they upset their Teenagers for not showing empathy towards them.

Most of the time, if you observe, this happens when the parents are present in the situations. In cases where the grandparents are spending time alone with the Teenagers, the issue does not arise. This is because of the expectations on the part of the either of the parents from both the parties. While the grandparents try to test their kid's loyalty towards their parenting techniques, the kids want to see if their parents love them more than their grandparents and can take their side. Hence, it is time for you to handle the situation very carefully and diplomatically. Try to avoid being there when there is an argument going on. Do not take either side and let them continue with their discussions. Stay calm and composed. The moment they realize, you are not taking either side, the show ends … cannot guess the ending though… but you will remain the hero of the show.

SUMMARY

In summary, the challenges that we faced as Teenagers in our generations are very meager when compared to those the current generations face. Some of the challenges are still the ones that we had to face as Teenagers. However, because of life and society has evolved enormously in the past few years, the impact of the challenges is much bigger in the current generation. Let us take a quick peep into what Teenager's life is revolving around:

1. Need for validation

2. Self-doubt

3. Fear of failure

4. Fear of rejection

5. Fear of judgment

6. Perfectionism

7. Procrastination

8. Low self-esteem

9. Low self-confidence

10. Peer pressure

11. Social pressure

12. Depression

13. Social media addiction

14. Grades

15. Parental conflicts

16. Bullying or violence at school

17. Popularity

18. Not having a friends circle

19. Boredom

20. Digitally distracted parents

21. Sedentary lifestyle

22. Drugs and abuse

23. Attraction to the opposite sex

24. ....

And the list goes on .... I work with Teenagers on these aspects individually in my program for them and try to provide solutions. But, let us move ahead with our journey and learn what, as parents, can you do to enkindle awareness as they say awareness is knowledge.

If we want our Teenagers to be happy and healthy individuals, we have to wake up from our deep sleep and get back to the basics. Yes, it is still possible. It is never too late to improve the relationship with a Teenager. Many families have seen improvements after weeks of implementing what I call the "Parenting Pie" recipe, which we will discuss in the coming chapters.

DOs Vs DONTs

When handling our Teenagers, we have to make sure we are aware of the things to do and not to do. I know the list is big, but we must understand what each point means and also try to apply them and watch the magic happen.

THINGS-TO-DO LIST

Establish boundaries and set expectations

Set limits and let them know you are the captain of the ship. Most of us try to become too lenient and forget to clarify family boundaries and behavioral expectations. Kids can surely express their opinions but they should also be conscious of the family rules and values that everyone has agreed on. This helps them know that irrespective of any tantrums they throw, a safety fence around them limits them. In addition, knowing that you are the head, though does not go well with them, they know that you are the driver and if things go wrong, you would be blamed and not them. This makes them feel more confident and secured.

Learn the Art of saying 'No' in a conducive manner

Some people refer to saying 'No' as Vitamin 'N'. Along with other multivitamins, children need a dosage of Vitamin 'N' too. During our childhood, after putting our request in front of our parents, we would be anxious and would wait to hear a 'Yes', keeping our fingers crossed. Well, gone are those days. Now, the children would never accept a 'No' for a reply. With Teenagers, it becomes all the more difficult as we are scared of the consequences of saying a No. This has resulted in Vitamin 'N' deficiency in Teenagers. While saying 'No', is not a bad thing, especially when it is required, we should learn the art of saying 'No'.

'No' is equivalent to a 'Yes' but with some conditions. You put forward the apprehensions that you have about saying yes in the form of conditions and let them accept that they would take care of these conditions while getting permission to do what they want to.

This way you are giving them the freedom as well as making sure you place restrictions on them.

Give full attention to them when they are talking

In the earlier generations, once the parent came back home from work or when parents were at home and not working, either way, there were no distractions and parents would be completely attentive and heard what the kids had to say. Now, with the work pressure building up and social media distractions coming into picture, most of the time we get distracted when the kids are trying to talk to us. This results in the kid being upset. If this keeps on repeating, then it might slowly result in our communication channel getting weaker between our Teenagers and us.

Whenever the Teen comes back from school or college and tries to speak to you, keep your stuff aside and give them a patient hearing. If you are in the middle of an important activity or task, just let them know and try to schedule a time when you can listen without any distractions. They feel happy as you are giving importance to them and their conversation.

Listen without judging or giving advice

Listening is healing; it is the basis of all talk therapies. Teenagers, who feel their parents listen and value their opinions, are more cooperative and less defiant. Try this simple suggestion, listen to your kid without making any judgement, without self-references, without advice and keep a close eye on your kid's responses. Chances are that he or she will share more and feel more comfortable turning to you for support.

I have been a bad listener all through my life. My dad always advised me not to react immediately and listen completely. I repeated the same mistake with my husband and with my kids too. I really get impatient, as I would not buy the discussion going on or I would end up continuing the conversation by filling words. I have now slowly trained myself to be a better listener. Most of the time, all that kids require is a listening wall, which does not react. So, the moment your Teenager comes to you with complaints or issues, become a wall, but do not forget to acknowledge with a few sighs like 'Umm', 'Is it', 'That's bad', 'I understand'. All that Teens need is empathy. If you have a strong opinion on the discussion, wait until the end of the discussion, and then express it indirectly in the form of a question.

Example:

Teen: *"Mom, you know what happened today. Svita was very mean to me ...."*

Mom: *"Oh is it'"….hmm….that's bad"* ……

Mom: *"Svita usually doesn't behave that way. You remember the lovely gift she gave you on your birthday. Why do you think she was abnormal today?"*

Teen *(after thinking for a while):* *"You know what Mom, just forget it. She must have been upset with what our Teacher did today. She punished her in front of the entire class. She could have called her separately to the Staffroom and warned her. I will call Svita now and ask her to cheer up."*

(End of the conversation)

In the above conversation, though Svita's mom knew her daughter was wrong, she did not try to stop her or intervene, trying to give her opinion. Instead, she waited for her daughter to finish and put an appropriate question, which made her realize the situation. This way Svita felt she was controlling the conversation and she decided to forgive her friend, not because her Mom had advised her to do so. Had it been the other way, Svita would have got agitated, upset and would have got up and left angrily.

Find a common topic to discuss regularly

Sometimes you need to find some common topics to discuss with your Teenager to change their moods and lighten the atmosphere. Make sure you do this on a regular basis to keep the bonding strong. Usually, fathers and sons often connect over sports, technology; mothers over gossip, dressing, movies, etc.

Once you know what these topics are, you can also use them to distract them from an intense argument. This is something, which I use as a savior for me each time. When there is a hot discussion going on in the family, between any of us or even between both my kids, I suddenly start a discussion regarding a topic of their interest, they get easily distracted, and then I heave a sigh of relief. I would like to give credit to my husband for this tip. He bonds very well with children and discusses regularly any topics that interest them. Well, I had to learn and practice this to get it naturally flowing within me.

Remember that you are the parent and you are the one who needs to be more calm and composed

Most of the time in crucial situations, we forget that we are the parents and behave as if we are another Teenager. We shout, we crib, and we moan and groan. Please do not forget that you are the matured one among both of you and it is your responsibility to be sensible enough to keep your anger under control. Try to be calm and composed. If you are a person who is short-tempered, my sincere advice to you is to do some breathing exercises and meditation to make sure you do not spoil your health dealing with these anger outbursts.

There are a lot of parents who have ended up having migraines, hypertension, etc. because they could not handle their Teenagers' tantrums. You have been into this world for more number of years than they have, you have more experience than they have, but it is not necessary to enforce these on them. Instead, with all the exposure and experience that you have, you should be strong enough to control your emotions and direct them into better ways of putting forward your point.

Be available, irrespective of the situation

Once a Dad and his Teenage daughter had a terrible fight over her dressing and there was a cold war going on between them. Both of them were so angry at each other that they did not speak for more than a week. On the following weekend, the kid suddenly realized that she had a pending project that had to be completed. She needed help and her Mom was out with her brother and would return late in the night. The only person she could turn towards for help was her Dad. Though it was tough for her, she approached her Dad and requested help. However, Dad's ego did not allow him to accept defeat. This really hurt the kid so bad that the cold war continued for many more days, months until some unfortunate incident occurred, and they both had to patch up.

Do you think you have to wait for some miracle to occur or some unfortunate incident to happen to drop off your so-called ego guards to connect back or be available to your kids? Irrespective of the past incidents, please abandon your ego and let your Teenager know that you are always available whenever she/he needs you.

Try to understand the exact cause behind their anger or outburst

Rahul comes home from college and goes into his room. His brother Rohan had come early from school and was inside the room, doing some activity. He lost his pen at school and so his mom advised him to use Rahul's pen. The moment Rahul sees Rohan using his pen; he snatches it from him and starts blasting him. Poor Rohan gets submissive and does not know how to react. When questioned, he tells about him losing the pen at school. Now Rahul gets madder and tells him that he is an irresponsible brat and does not value things. Their mom tries to intervene, but Rahul gets angry saying mom always takes Rohan's side.

His mom just asks Rohan to come out of his room, makes him apologize and takes him away to another room. She consoles him and makes him understand that Rahul might be upset about something.

After some time, she makes Rahul's favorite milkshake and enters his room. She sees him sleeping and massages his head lightly. Rahul breaks down, puts his head in his mother's lap, and starts sobbing. His mom has never seen him cry in the past few years and gets shocked. Rahul apologizes for his bad behavior and tells her that his scholarship exam results were out and he lost it just by one mark. This upset him and resulted in the outrageous behavior with his younger brother for just a small thing as using his pen.

This is the case with most of the Teenagers. What we see is sometimes not the real reason for their anger and outburst. In the background, there might be a strong root cause, which we as a parent should try to get it out from them. This is possible only if you remain calm and composed and allow them to settle down and behave as if nothing had happened. They will feel guilty for their misbehavior; and will reveal the real root cause themselves. Most of the time, there might not be a reason for you to question them.

Help them find ways to relieve their anger and stress

Get your Teens registered in any physical activity that they like or enjoy. Make them learn some instrument. Engage them in a sport, an extra-curricular activity, playing an instrument. Turn into their best friends when they search for some 'ME' time away from parents and family. This will help them relieve themselves of their anger and help them reduce their stress levels. Some of the Teenagers enjoy listening to music, playing an instrument, dancing, etc. Make sure you make arrangements accordingly at home so that when they try to stay inside their cocoon for a while, they have some company inside that cocoon.

Give them space and respect their privacy but be watchful

As I mentioned above, every Teenager needs some 'ME' time and this is a good thing. Some Teenagers, when angry or upset, suddenly go silent for a while. We can never guess what is going on in their mind. Do not try to question their behavior. There could be some battle going on. In some situations, they want to be with themselves; to try to figure out stuff. They might be chatting with their friends on their devices. Give some respect to their privacy and give them some space. Do not try to poke questions at them.

However, be watchful, as parents, you always need to have something called an 'Eagle's view'. Be mindful of what the Teen is going through. Sometimes it could be a warning signal too. Though you do not want to break their privacy, talk to their friends or teachers. Try to figure out, if you need to be concerned about something. Then go ahead and have a quick friendly conversation with your Teen.

Get them involved in the family decisions

Involving your Teenager in your family decisions boosts their confidence levels and helps them differentiate between what is right and what is wrong. You stand a fair chance of reduced anger or outbursts since they now know that you trust them and feel they are capable enough to take charge of things.

If you are unable to let them take the final decision, open up a debate with your Teenager and let them express why they think their decision is right. Put forward your point along with the justification you have. This way, they would learn to understand the possibility of different choices and the consequences of choosing each one of them. Give them a chance and see; they will surprise you with the justifications for their choices. Even though you lose, you will feel confident that your Teenager can take some good and sensible decisions independently in their lives.

Let them do regular house chores

Make sure your Teenager has a regular house chore routine. This is important to make them feel grounded irrespective of any situation at home. They also bond with the family and siblings if they are doing something together. I make sure my kids set the table together before dinner. Even if they would have fought a little while ago, they know they have to work together and divide the activity between them. This does sometimes end up in breaking the ice between both of them.

Divide the chores equally among the kids, parents, and set some rules against it. They do not have to finish their chores feeling miserable or serious. Let them play some music and enjoy it while doing. Come up with some funny ideas. Let them get some chores, which they like, and some, which they do not. This way they will learn to adjust in situations that are not favorable to them.

Inspire instead of instructing them

A few days ago, when I was travelling to Delhi, there was a family of four, Mom and her 3 kids seated in front of me. One was a Teenager, the other a middle-school kid and the last one was a toddler. The moment they finished their lunch, each one of them took out some book from their bags and enjoyed reading. This surprised everyone around. There were so many kids, who were on their mobiles, playing games. Their parents were asking them to play instead of watching videos online, but the kids never bothered to listen to their parent's instructions.

Most of the times, the kids and especially the Teenagers observe the parent's behavior a lot. What you cannot do by giving instructions, you can inspire them by doing it yourself. Inspire them to show gratitude, to serve society, to be happy, to dream big, and to bounce back after a failure. What they see you doing is what they get inspired to do.

Become a role model

Parents are the role models for children. My Dad was my hero and he always remains one. Each time I try to reach to his expectations, he surpasses it. Well, of course, not to make me feel inferior but to push me even harder. People need a role model, a mentor, whom they can look up to and feel proud to follow them.

If you happen to be that person for your Teenager, then that is the best thing you can give to him/her as a parent. This will sidestep wrong company or influences.

Appreciate often

Every Teenager is unique and has some spark in them. Appreciate your Teenager for who they are and make sure you do it at every opportunity you get. Teenagers generally tend to have low self-esteem as they are trying to look for validation everywhere around them. Receiving appreciation for their small victories will boost their morale to the extent you can never imagine. Their confidence levels reach the peaks and they keep pushing their targets much higher without your intervention.

I suggest parents in my program to use some tools that I suggest to appreciate and celebrate. This has really helped the parents and Teenagers connect with each other happily.

Be humorous

Remember those days when you jumped around, acting like a monkey to impress your little toddler. Now is the time to get back your same funny side. The only difference is you do not have to jump up or down to make them laugh, you just have to crack some more matured funny situational jokes in front of your Teenager. Remember not to choose some silly ones; you might just end up making them furious instead of getting happy.

It comes naturally to some, but if you are a stubborn, serious parent... then it is time to change dear. Nothing can lighten up the mood of your Teenager better than a funny joke or narrating a funny incident. It might sound silly...but yes, .it works. Try it out and repeat it as many times as you can and enjoy.

Eat meals together

I recommend all the parents to have a family mealtime together without any distractions. Dining area is the place we get to share stuff, discuss, debate and laugh. Try not to have any distractions like TV, movie going on, etc. Instead, you can have some light music playing to give an ambience and atmosphere of a restaurant.

Have regular family outings

Family outings are the best places to create a great bonding among the family members. It is also a chance for your Teenager to drop off their stress levels and be ready to bounce back to their regular routine. You can plan for either customized tours or group tours. Group tours help your Teenager to mingle with other people. These will help them improve their social skills and refresh them. Sometimes Teenagers get bored of spending all the time with their family members.

Nature is surely a great healer. Plan for places, which are closer to nature. You can also try to include an activity like trekking, yoga or meditation as part of the trip. This will help your Teenager unwind and feel refreshed.

Encourage their interests and passions

Teenage years also happen to be crucial years for studies. However, encourage your Teenager to pursue some passion or interest apart from their regular studies. Discuss with them about how much time they get to spend on their interests. Do not put too many restrictions and force the Teenagers to only study. Focusing on academics surely is going to be the first priority, but they also need some stress busters in the form of their interests or passions.

Allow sibling time without intervention

If your Teenager has a sibling, allow them to spend some time with each other. Make sure you are away from the scene; else, they might end up fighting, trying to grab your attention. Instead of fun time, it might end up in fight time. My kids bond well when they are watching any cartoon show or movie together. They laugh their hearts out and that makes me too laugh from my bedroom.

If your Teenager is the elder one, you can assign the responsibility of helping the younger one in their studies, some activity or a project. Ask them to go out shopping together and get something. These are the moments where they connect with each other and will help avoid any sibling-rivalry among them.

There are many more such subtle things that you can do, to make sure your Teenager connects with you and with your family in a better way.

THINGS NOT-TO-DO LIST

Now let us look at the common mistakes that we parents make when handling our Teenagers.

Talking to them like kids

Your Teenager is moving towards adulthood and so they expect the respect that an adult gets. Though they do not demand it directly, they feel happy when you treat them like an adult. Do not crack silly jokes and expect them to laugh. Do not try to cajole them as you did when they were younger. Be mindful of what you speak in front of their social circle, their friends, teachers, etc.

They carry a lot of self-respect, so one small mistake and you might have to pay for it. Talk to them like friends when required, take their opinions, involve them, discuss and debate with them. They sometimes have better logic and justification. Eventually, you might end up changing your perspective about many things.

Blaming and accusing

Stop blaming your Teenager. When Teenagers are accused, they become defensive. When you give them information, simply and respectfully, they will more likely assume responsibility for what they have to do.

There might be situations where the behavior of the Teenager or the negligence of the Teenager has affected someone else. In such situations, do not directly start accusing them for their mistakes. Instead, share with them, the consequences of their actions; and how it has affected others. Awareness results in realization. This will make them feel more responsible when they get into a similar situation next time.

Victimizing

Most of the parents have a habit or rather a hobby of complaining about their Teenager. At every opportunity, they whine, lament, to friends or relatives—at home and in public. Such negativity weakens a parent's leadership at home and breeds a toxic environment. It is also terrible role modeling. If you complain about your kid, your kid will complain about you—and that is a dead-end for everyone.

Punishing

Punishments have no place in a caring relationship. Teenagers are averse to punishments. We are all humans and to err is human. If a mistake results in a realization and learning, then there is no necessity for punishment. Try to find alternatives to punishment. You try to state your feelings, expectations and show ways to amend their mistakes. Offer choices to them and let them take action on it.

Many parents see discipline and punishment as the same. The problem with punishment is that it makes it too easy for a Teenager to ignore their misdeed and focus instead on how unreasonable the parent is. In addition, it deprives the Teenager of the work they need to do to become more mature and more responsible. For real change to take place, our Teenagers need to do their emotional homework. Punishment interferes with that important process.

Worrying about small stuff and ignoring the big ones

Most of the time, the parents might not be in approval of the Teenager's decision, about their dressing, haircut, not taking part in a play, etc. Before you start complaining look at the big picture. If it is not putting your child at risk, give them the freedom to make age-appropriate decisions themselves and learn the consequences from their choices. Do not try to become their shields and protect them from pain, disappointment or failure. Protecting them from the realities of life takes away valuable learning opportunities before they are out on their own.

You would still be there for guidance and support, but step back and let them take the lead. Just let your child know that you are there for them.

Watch out for things, which might be more serious. Toxic friendship, depression, drugs, addiction to life-threatening games are the ones where you need to put your foot down, set rules and make the Teen adhere to it. Also, try to understand that you have to handle these situations with extreme delicacy. If you feel you are not able to handle them by yourself, get help immediately. Delay in such situations has resulted in untoward incidents. Please….. get help immediately.

Too much or too little discipline

Discipline is a good thing to have when it is in the right quantity. Trying to discipline your child due to anger or frustration is not the right approach. At the same time, trying to be lenient and let go of rules because of their tantrums, is also not an alternative option.

Set rules in the house and explain the reason for setting them. Become a self-example by adhering to it and formulate the consequences of breaking the rules. This will make them appreciate the discipline of the house. Mealtimes, chore assignment, social obligations are some of the rules which every family member has to follow.

Name-calling / Making a prophecy

Do not use words that hurt your Teenagers especially in front of others. Instead, you can question, and let them take up the ownership of their mistake. You can try to make it humorous too, to sound less offensive.

Do not indulge in making a prophecy for your Teenagers. Sometimes prophecies do come true! Keeping the humor part of it aside, it really jolts the belief system of your Teen. They start believing that what you said is what is going to happen with them. Repetition of this is going to plunge their self-confidence levels to the lowest. Think before you put words in your mouth.

Forcing them into activities that you choose / Taking decision on their behalf

Any activity that you involve your Teenager in should be on consensus and approval. Do not force things on to them. Try to understand their likes and interests. If they have an issue in agreeing to what you say, ask them to explain their perspective and check if they do have some valid reason.

The same applies to the decisions already taken. You need to be more sensitive to your Teenager's decisions and choices. Making them capable, enough to take decisions and bear the consequences of it will make them take charge of their life and face failure. You need to prepare your kids for the worst and be independent when they are out of your nest.

Lecturing and Moralizing / Comparing with others

Too many advises, morals and comparisons make the Teenagers become stronger as rebels. Having open discussions, showing empathy and getting to know their side of the story is what involves them and makes them willing to share things with us. Be conscious of what you are doing when dealing with their feelings.

Criticizing their friends

Teenagers are very particular about their peer group. Friends and friendships give them a sense of belonging, a feeling of being valued and help in developing their confidence. They give utmost importance to their friend than their families. If you do not like your Teenager's friends, criticizing their friends will make their bond stronger with the same friends. Realize that criticizing your Teen's friends is like criticizing an aspect of your child. Instead, make clear statements about their behavior.

When your Teen starts changing because of the kids he/she is hanging out with, use a structure parenting routine of setting limits and managing the time they spend together.

Some of the Do's and Don'ts come naturally to a few parents. It all depends on the internal wiring of the parents to handle the situations. Most of the parents struggle in trying out the above tips. In my program, parents can understand their internal wiring system and accordingly create a customized '***Parenting Blueprint***' for themselves.

THE
PARENTING
RECIPE

Parenting — Visualize It Like A Recipe

G ood parenting is the greatest gift you can give to your child. Not all parents know how to do it. By learning or improving your parenting skills, you can become a wonderful parent and a wonderful role model. I have seen many parents arguing about parenting, if it is a natural phenomenon, art or a science. Parenting according to me, is neither an Art, to learn, nor Science to teach. Parenting is like a recipe, which requires the basic ingredients, which are an important part of the recipe. You can later customize it as per your requirements. When it becomes a recipe, it becomes easy for anyone to learn it, master it and customize it.

The other rationale on which I compare it with a recipe is because the moment we look at parenting as a recipe, the burden that you have been carrying on your head about all the issues that you are currently facing, just vanishes. With the advent of technology surging into our lifestyles, many of us research a lot of recipes online and keep trying them out in our kitchen to please ourselves, or our family. The first time we try it, even though we stick to the ingredients mentioned in the recipe, we may end up getting it wrong. Then we keep trying it repeatedly, until it becomes a practice and we have mastered it.

The next phase that comes is when the family or the chef of the family feels that we can make some modifications to the ingredients, measure of the ingredients or the method of cooking to appeal more to the family. Here comes the customization. There are different versions of any standard recipe. As an example, if you take a toast, there are so many varieties of toasts that we can make - Grilled potato toast, French toast, Masala cheese French toast, regular vegetarian toast ... and so on. My mouth is already watering thinking about all these. Therefore, there is variety and even in that variety, you may decide to either eat it in the normal way or grill it. In addition to all these, you can add the toppings that tickle your Teenager's taste buds.

In grasping this concept of a recipe, it would definitely take us some time. All this while, we considered parenting as something that comes naturally and so transitioning to the new idea will definitely face a lot of resistance from our conscience and our old belief system. However, as I mentioned earlier, to innovate and to adapt ourselves to new concepts has been the secret of survival for any living being. So is with this concept of parenting too. After we overcome the resistance from our own self, we might face the resistance from the family members too, as it is a new recipe and they are not used to tasting it. However, a good parent never gives up if they consider that the recipe is healthy and is essential for the wellbeing of the family.

WHY A PIE?

Now that we have an understanding of why I have compared parenting to a recipe, let us further progress our journey and see why I am talking about a Pie and not any other dish. 'Pie' is used as a metaphor in many cases and in most of the areas of life for comparison. This is probably because it refers to something wholesome. I am talking about it not as a metaphor but with strong intentions.

"A PIE is a baked dish which is usually made of a pastry dough casing that completely contains a filling of various sweet or savory ingredients."

Most of the Teenagers like bakery items. Some of the girls start getting health conscious but there are a few days called the 'Cheat Days' when they are ready to break the rules. Personally as a parent, I would like my Teenager to eat healthily, as these are the years of rapid growth and development. As much important it is for the parents to give their child a balanced diet, it is equally important to allow them to have those junk days when they can satisfy their cravings to eat junk. Too much is too bad, and so we need to set rules on this too.

The PIE has a crust and soft ingredients inside. The combination of the crust and the soft ingredients, (which can be altered), as per our taste and necessity, enhances the rationale for choosing it. For a parent, to adopt the Parenting Pie model, he/she needs to understand the importance of the crust and its soft ingredients. Crust, in this case, would be those strict boundaries that you want to enforce in your parenting while the soft ingredients could be those subtle parenting skills that you would like to incorporate to make your Teenager fall in love with the taste of the Pie.

BASIC INGREDIENTS OF A PARENTING PIE FOR TEENAGERS

Let us now look at the basic ingredients that are required for creating the Parenting Pie. These ingredients are not something that I randomly picked up myself. I arrived at these ingredients after going through the incidents shared by other parents in my survey. There were some beautiful Life Lessons learnt by the parents from their Teenagers.

The below basic ingredients are very important for your parenting. Irrespective of your parenting style, I recommend to include them to make your Pie, tasty, durable and appealing to you and your Teenager.

INGREDIENTS FOR CRUST

The following are the basic ingredients for the crust, which are necessary to make it seal all the ingredients of the filling. If the binding is not proper and tasty, the recipe will not turn out to be good. Thickness of the crust is also very important to make sure there is a proper proportion between the hard and soft part of the baked pie.

The crust ingredients are crucial in the context of parenting pie, because the entire essence of parenting lies in them. Let us discuss each one of them in detail as they form an important base for a PIE.

- Trust/Confidence

- Discipline

- Family Values

Incident

Richa, for the first time, got access to a smartphone. She had moved to high school recently and had made some new friends. All her friends had accounts on Instagram and Richa felt left out. She knew her parents had given her the phone to be able to discuss stuff about school with her friends on WhatsApp. However, due to the peer pressure, she let a friend of her create an account for her on Instagram. She started using it for a while, in the process got requests from some unknown people and started chatting with them. However, all this was making her feel uneasy, as she was brought up in an environment where TRUST was an important ingredient in the relationship. She slowly became submissive and started avoiding her parents.

Richa's mom and dad knew that there was something definitely troubling her. Her mom checked her phone and found out what the issue was. However, they trusted her and waited for her to come out on her own. One day finally, Richa shared the entire episode with her mom and burst out crying. Her mom first consoled her and appreciated her for sharing it with her. She then advised her about the pros and cons of using social media. She also warned her by sharing a few stories of the consequences of using it in a wrong manner. This boosted her morale and Richa, on her own, the next day, disabled her account on Instagram. She did not give in to peer pressure of enabling it back. Instead, she used WhatsApp to connect with her friends. After a few years, when she felt confident enough to handle social media, she enabled her account. Now her Mom and others have also joined Instagram and are on her friend's list.

Trust/Confidence

Trust and Confidence are like the All Purpose Flour that helps in binding the other ingredients of the crust.

Through the Teenage years, one of the most important things in parenting is developing trust in your relationship with your kids. Your Teenager needs your trust to help them in their transition to adulthood. However, this trust needs to be mutual. A relationship without trust leads to questioning each other's honesty. When your children were younger, they probably trusted you unconditionally. However, when they grow up and become more independent, they start to notice and question more. It is around this time that your Teen may notice whether you do what you say, which is a key factor in building trust. As a parent, you cannot demand trust. It is a gradual process, which requires mutual commitment and will inevitably strengthen your relationship. It will also let your child develop healthy relationships based on trust in the future. It is worth noting that Teenagers are going through an intensely private time in their lives. Personal space becomes very important to them, so the desire for privacy does not always mean that an untrustworthy activity is taking place. It is important to keep this in mind.

It requires a great deal of personal restraint, fighting through parental fears, and having faith in them, that they have been taught correctly, and will act accordingly. If there has been any incident when your Teen has violated your trust, try to remain calm. I know this is something easier said than done. When you feel like your Teen has betrayed your trust, it is only natural to feel angry, disappointed and concerned for your Teen.

While it is completely okay to feel these things, it will not help your cause if you choose to let strong emotions dictate your response. As a parent, you need to respond in a calm and rational manner. By keeping your cool, you will be able to keep the focus of the conversation on the issue and your kid's behavior. If your response resembles a confrontation or emotional outburst, you will end up with an unproductive argument and power struggle.

Children and Teenagers are more inclined to lie to their parents if they are fearful of an angry or hostile response. As a parent, you want to encourage and affirm honesty and openness in the Parent-Teen relationship. Overreactions and angry outbursts tend to create distrust rather than foster trust. This does not mean parents should not take such issues seriously. However, a serious response is different from an angry and hostile reaction.

Incident

Sameer has been an explorer from his childhood. He likes experimenting with new stuff and satisfying his inquisitive desires. He had a good friend-circle and enjoyed being together all the time after school. One day while returning from school, he met Peter uncle, an old man in his 60s and a good friend of his grandfather. Peter had no kids and so was fond of Sameer and his group. That day Peter warned them against visiting the old bungalow in the town outskirts. The kids grew curious and decided to visit the bungalow after dinner that night.

Sameer's dad was a God-fearing and disciplined person who worked as a Manager in the Town's bank. Sameer's mother had passed away a few years back and so his Dad was raising him as a single father. He played the role of both mother and a father, but when it came to discipline; he knew it was required for him to set the rules. Sameer tried to resist many of the regulations but had no choice other than to follow what his Dad said.

That night after dinner, Sameer's father was busy checking some accounts. Sameer sneaked out quietly but his father saw his shadow moving out of the gate when he looked out of his window. He immediately followed him on his cycle and caught him on the way. Without questioning him, why he wriggled out, he just mentioned that it was against the rules of the house to go out in the night without his permission. Sameer pleaded but his dad did not give in. Dad insisted Sameer to march back home and can do whatever he wants to do the next day morning. Sameer reluctantly went back home cursing his Dad.

The next day morning when he reached his school, he heard something that shocked him to the core. Even though he did not accompany, his friends did make a visit to the old bungalow the previous night. There were some illegal activities happening in the bungalow. The people there were armed. Suddenly there was a raid by the police and kids had to hide themselves. When they tried to escape, the police presumed the kids to be a part of the gang and shot one of his friends. His friend was now in the hospital recovering and his other friends were still in a state of shock. They felt glad that Sameer did not have to witness this unfortunate incident.

Sameer immediately ran to his father's bank and shared the entire incident with him. He thanked him several times for making sure he stuck to the rules and acknowledged that now he had understood the importance of Discipline. He also promised his dad that he would, from now on, willingly follow the rules and guidelines set by him.

Discipline

Discipline is another important ingredient, which is like the combination of the Salt and Sugar in the crust. Without this, the crust might be tasteless.

Disciplining a Teen can be very frustrating. The truth is that, it's your Teen's job to push the boundaries. They are becoming independent, trying to figure out what is correct, and what is not. It is your job as a parent to demarcate the boundaries. Teens today need as well as desire discipline (although they would never admit it). Your kids will appreciate later in their life that you drew the line of discipline and more so if you did it in a way not to impact the relationship. Discipline is going to help your Teenager get to a place where they want to be and keeping them away from where they do not want to be. If your Teen understands that you are disciplining them for their own good, they will ultimately understand. They will not like the consequences, and may get upset with you temporarily, but they will come to realize that they are bringing the consequences upon themselves, and that is when their behavior changes.

Parents can use various approaches to discipline Teen. Many books refer to two kinds of parenting in the context of discipline. Specifically, while the words "authoritarian" and "authoritative" are similar, authoritarian parenting is very different from authoritative parenting.

Authoritarian parents typically choose punishment vs. discipline. Specifically, they value obedience and believe that children are naturally strong-willed and self-indulgent. Thus, they use punishment as a way to break the will of the child. Hence, Teens do not have the opportunity to learn self-discipline or self-regulation. As a result, Teens with authoritarian parents tend to be depressed and have lower self-esteem than those with authoritative parents.

Authoritative parents, on the other hand, set clear limits and rules, and enforce consequences. However, they communicate with their Teens and are willing to negotiate. Furthermore, they respect their child's rights and opinions. Therefore, Teens with authoritative parents feel supported but not suppressed.

The important point to note here is that the Teenagers need to be able to accept and give permission to their parents to discipline them. Most of the time, this will automatically happen if the Teen likes and respects the parent. There might be very few chances of turning into a rebel in such cases. So, to include this ingredient as a part of your parenting, it might be a good idea to gain that liking and respect from your kids from their childhood itself. Though it is difficult to gain this in their Teenage years, it is not an impossible task.

Incident

Keertana was slowly growing into a beautiful Teenager. There were many boys in her college, wanting to have a chat with her. Though this made her feel important, she tried to ignore them always. Keertana's mother was a nurse in a hospital. Her dad worked in a private firm. She had a younger brother Anil who was 10 years old. Her parents always volunteered at the blind school every weekend to tell stories to the students and entertain them. She would take care of her brother on that day. One weekend, her parents had to travel, as one of their close relatives was ill. They informed the school that they cannot come this weekend and asked the school to find some volunteers from outside. They left Keertana and Anil with one of their friends and left. Keertana felt bad that their parents had to leave disappointed for not volunteering at school. She knew that her aunt would not allow her either.

The next day on her way to college, she found the same gang of boys who wanted to chat with her, sitting at a tea stall, tittle-tattling. An idea hatched in her mind and she approached them. The boys got scared, as they thought she was going to question them. However, they felt relieved when she addressed them with respect. She spoke to them about the blind school and convinced them to volunteer that week instead of her parents. The boys were glad to help and went there on the weekend. Upon return, her parents got to know about the boys volunteering during the weekend. They really felt proud of their daughter as she managed to keep up their values of serving the society. From the next week onwards, Keertana's family along with the boys volunteered at the blind schools and slowly this message spread across. Eventually, all the blind schools in that district had students volunteering during the weekends.

The District collector visited one of the schools for the Independence Day celebrations and was impressed to hear the inspiring story. He rewarded Keertana that day and also, in his speech, encouraged all the parents of the students to make values a part of their parenting. Keertana's parents really felt proud of their upbringing and understood the importance of values. They were always scared to send Keertana alone or leave her alone at home and were very restrictive on where she goes. However, that day they understood that if you give good values to your children, they know how to handle freedom in a positive and impactful way instead of misusing it.

Family Values

Values grow out of our experiences with others, including the culture in which we live, our friends and our family. Parents' values have the greatest effect on children. Therefore, parents must be sure to know what their own values are and make sure they feel proud to pass on those beliefs to their children. Parents should talk to their Teens about what they believe and about other's values – it is important to encourage Teen's confidence in their own values while at the same time respecting the values of others.

There is no single better way to teach than by exemplifying. Children of all ages learn by imitating, and they are very adept at picking up the differences between what you say and what you do. So if you want to teach honesty, be honest. Do not lie when turning down a commitment because you do not want to hurt the other person's feelings – your children will learn that it is okay to lie in some cases. If you want your children to be giving and unselfish, find ways to volunteer or help others. We must show what it means to be a compassionate, respectful, honest and generous adult. It is our job as parents and caregivers to be the stable moral compass on the shoreline, the lighthouse, from which they can measure their behaviors.

Do not make the mistake of only talking about values when something goes wrong. Nothing will turn your Teens off more than preaching values to them after they have made a mistake. Talk to them when everyone is relaxed, and do it in a light, conversational manner. When values are a frequent topic in your house, Teens will understand that they are important. They will not show any signs of acceptance or acknowledgement. Never expect them to. But definitely, it gets registered in their mind. All that you can do is store enough and relevant examples and information in their brain. They will surely retrieve the relevant ones when it is time for it.

INGREDIENTS FOR FILLING

The ingredients for filling are as important as the crust but these require the help of the crust ingredients to give them a shape. We have to make sure all the ingredients are in the right measure. The measure of the ingredients can keep changing based on your Teenager, atmosphere at your house, atmosphere at the Teen's school and the Teen's social circle.

With the basic ingredients, you cannot come up with the right measure at the first shot. You might have to keep experimenting, changing the measure and reviewing the results. Of course, mastering a recipe for the first time itself, is not an easy job, don't you agree? So, play around with these basic ingredients, as there is no specific order to add them but of course, there is a necessity for these to be a part of your parenting pie. I did meet parents who argue that all ingredients mentioned here are not necessary for their recipe. Well, going by generic needs and by large, most of the conflicts between parents and Teenagers, these are the ones, which are supposed to be a part of the basic ingredients. I have no issues if you still buy to differ. After all, you are the Teen's parent and have every right to make decisions. However, I would still recommend you to add these basic ingredients in your parenting and watch how the results differ. In addition, there might be some overlap with some of the ingredients. Few of the parents might feel that one ingredient combines the quality of two or more.

Would you not like to try it out for yourself and see!

- UNCONDITIONAL LOVE
- EMPATHY
- PATIENCE
- TRANSPARENCY
- APPRECIATION
- COMMUNICATION
- OPEN MIND
- ENCOURAGEMENT
- UNDERSTANDING
- FRIENDSHIP
- EDUCATION ON SEX / ALCOHOL / DRUGS / ABUSE
- EMPOWERMENT
- INSPIRATION
- HUMOR

Incident

Roger was a great swimmer. However, he had become lazy as a Teenager. He was the favorite of his Coach. He got selected to participate for a State level Championship. The tournament had two levels and one had to clear both of them to apply for a National level championship. The Government was also offering a scholarship to the selected students for their academics until they complete their Post-graduation. A lot of students looked forward to be a part of this championship. Roger was excited too. But, then came the announcement that whoever cleared Level 1 will have to attend the swimming refresher classes in the summer vacation. And, this came as a shock to Roger. Roger was so much looking forward to his summer vacation as he just needed a break and wanted to relax. He went back home that day and discussed with his parents. His parents asked him to first attempt his Level 1 instead of worrying about his vacation and he agreed.

Not willingly, but he attempted his Level 1. He was expecting not to clear it so that his vacation remained undisturbed. His coach and parents had so much confidence in him. However, unlike his expectations, he cleared his first level. Roger remained silent, while his family, school friends and his coach were elated with his victory and were celebrating. A few more students cleared Level 1 from his school. That night, there was a terrible argument between Roger and his Dad. Roger was not willing to cancel or postpone his vacation. He wanted to appear for Level II but was unwilling to attend the summer classes. Upon knowing Roger's intent, his Dad went mad over him, as he felt this was a God-given opportunity for him to get the scholarship but Roger was in no mood to listen. Going to the classes would have helped him practice well.

His parents were terribly upset, so they discussed about it and decided to go with his choice. Roger enjoyed his vacation and the following month participated in Level II. He missed the selection by merely 5 seconds. This made him realize his mistake and he felt his parents are going to hate him for life. However, when he came back home that day, his parents congratulated him on his performance. Though he had not cleared his Level II, they were happy to have realized the caliber their son had. With no preparation at all, he just missed it by 5 seconds was all that they discussed during the entire dinner. Roger was really upset and felt he was blessed to have such understanding parents. He made a decision for Life, not to repeat this mistake of his and to abide by what his parents decide for him.

His parents, his coach saw a great shift in his attitude. He was no more a lazy person and practiced daily. The following year, he got an opportunity to participate in a National level championship directly and made his parents proud by winning the Gold medal. He is now training to represent his country in the International tournaments.

Unconditional Love

We might have to struggle a bit to include this ingredient. Most of the time, giving Love is based on how happy we are with our Teen at that moment. It is easy to say we love our children when they are being good. However, what our Teens need is love which is given with no strings attached; where there is no expectation of being loved in return. Unconditional love gives the children the assurance that everything is going to be fine in the end. Even when we dislike or disapprove of their behaviors, our children must always know that we stand beside them.

Parents usually try to react to bad situations without thinking of the long-run association that we are going to have with our children. The moment there is a conflict, we give up on our patience, compassion, expertise and experience. All that we see is how hurtful those emotions of ours are. While most of us hate being in these situations, we will surely have to face them regularly when dealing with our Teenagers. We believe and decide that things are not going to be normal between us anymore. We fail to understand the importance of giving unconditional love in those situations.

When your Teenager is going through a difficult phase physically and mentally, there are cases when they react badly or take some wrong decisions. It is at this moment that they need to understand that you have forgiven them and are ready to move ahead. This gives them a sense of security and they start opening up with you. They work consciously on the flaws that they might be having. Please remember that unconditional love is one of the long-term investments to make sure everything is going to end well with positive results. Without this ingredient in your parenting, this phase is going to get tough for both you and your Teen with no positive changes in them even in the long run.

Conversation

Rita hated social studies and her Mom did not like this at all. Rita's mom is a postgraduate in Social Sciences. Following is the conversation that goes on between both of them.

Rita: *"I am desperately waiting for the school to get over this year. Next year I am going to college and will never require studying Social studies once again."*

Mom: *"What is so wrong about Social studies that you hate it so much?"*

Rita: *"Anil sir is a terrible teacher. He hates Smitha and me so much. He does not leave a single chance to embarrass us in front of the class."*

Mom: *"Did something happen in the class, which makes you think he hates you both?"*

Rita: *"He made me stand up in the class today to answer some questions from a lesson that he taught us two weeks back. How can one remember it after so many days? When I gave a wrong answer, everyone started giggling silently and Anil sir joined too."*

Mom (after trying to feel her daughter's emotions):

"Rita, it sounds as if you really felt embarrassed giving a wrong reply in front of the entire class. That must have been difficult for you. I really understand."

Rita: *"Yes, I really felt like a dumb. I really do not feel like going to the next Social class. All my friends must be thinking I am such an idiot."*

Mom: *"I think you are very smart. Not sure if you believe it though."*

Rita: *"I do my homework daily but I get scared when I am asked to answer in front of the entire class."*

Mom: *"Now I get it, it is actually not because you hate Social studies as a subject but because you do not like Anil sir asking you questions in front of the class."*

Empathy (Listen But Decide As A Parent)

Showing Empathy is a way of connecting with your Teen. It shows they know they are experiencing something… even if you do not understand exactly how it feels to them. The message that they are not alone and you understand their feelings, is very important for them to hear. When they feel understood and supported, they are more likely to stay motivated. Your empathy can help them become self-aware and be able to speak up for what they need. Kindly understand that empathy is not the same as showing sympathy. Sympathy lowers the expectations, but you do not have to do that with empathy. You can validate your child's feelings and still hold high standards.

Teens usually give nonverbal hints about how they are feeling or what is the challenge that they are going through. It is very important that you understand and be sensitive to those feelings. You need to give them a chance to speak out or vent out their frustration without judging them or interrupting them. Any frustrations that you have because of their earlier behavior have to be set aside. Just try to visualize the situation or the incident by stepping in their shoes. I am sure you, as a parent, would have either not given it the importance given by them. Nevertheless, stand by them and hear them out. When starting a dialogue with them try using the word 'I' more often than 'You'. The moment you utter the word, 'You', they start getting more defensive.

Based on the situation, parents try to intervene to give a solution to the problem that their Teen is facing or try to take his/her side and approach the required people to fix it. While we are trying to take the side of our Teenager in terms of feeling what he/she is feeling, it is not required to react to the situation and take action immediately. Listen like a friend, think like a Teen but act like a parent. Most of the time, parents cannot handle the negative emotion of their Teen. While trying to empathize with them, they end up feeling emotional about the entire situation and react instead of responding.

If the incident pertains to something which happened outside your house, after showing empathy towards your Teen, always take a break, step away for some time and try to look at the situation from a parent's angle and then decide how you need to respond to the situation. Think about what to talk to the Teen before starting a dialogue. Ask appropriate questions in a manner they realize the true essence of the incident and the reason why the things happened that way. Ask them to choose what they would like to do now. Offer different choices and the consequences of each of those. Most of the time, all that the kids want is to share the incident with someone and relax their mind. When you make them the owner and controller of the result of the action, they realize that maybe there is nothing that needs to be done at all. So, all you need to do is feel the way they do, share your feelings, and then have a dialogue as a parent.

Incident

Susanne is a single mother of three children; Richa who is 16 years old, Ricky 10 and Ronn 5. She recently lost her husband and the family was trying to get over the loss. She became a full-time mother after her first daughter was born. Her husband worked as a senior-level executive in a private firm. Being at home, completely dedicating herself to her kids was her decision. However, losing her husband made her change her decision. She was an MBA postgraduate from a reputed college, and that helped her get her husband's job after he lost his life in a car accident. Financially, the family was now taken care of. However, things did not remain the same at home after that. She tried getting help from different caretakers but the kids would drive them away with their fights. Especially Richa hated anyone to be at home other than her family.

Every day was a different challenge to managing things at home and at work. Richa, in spite of being the eldest, did not understand her Mom's plight. In fact, things were getting more challenging because of her Teenage tantrums. Every day at the dinner table, she would provoke either Ricky or Ronn and try to pick up an argument with them. She tried to boss over them and they were not ready to accept it. Ronn would end up crying but Ricky would fight back. After a tiring day at the office, Susanne would feel totally worn out. She would really go crazy when she saw kids getting in a row and without knowing how to handle it, she would just yell at Richa for being so insensitive. Then would go and lock herself up in the room without having her dinner. The kids would then calm down. This kept on repeating until one day when she saw Ronn, the little one, yelling at everyone and then walking out of the dining room and going to his room and locking himself up. All this while, Susanne thought that she was able to calm her children with her temper and behavior. However, what she saw was that instead of teaching them a lesson, her kids were trying to imitate her and picked up her behavior. This really troubled her.

She tried to take help from a parenting coach as advised by her friend. The first step that she was asked to do was to deal with her Teenager in a more patient way. This sounded near to impossible for her. So, she took the help of the coach and enrolled for a meditation class twice a week close to her office. At home, the situations repeated, but this time she decided to be a much calmer person. Instead of yelling at Richa, she supported her against Ricky and Ronn. She told them both, Richa is your elder sister and so she tries to trigger you both or provoke you to check if you can face the situation when the other kids do this with you in school or neighborhood." Richa was shocked to see this change in her mother's behavior and did not know how to react.

Each time Richa triggered her Mom, she handled the situation in a more patient manner. Richa started feeling guilty over her behavior with her mother. She realized the pain that her mother was going through after having lost her husband. The fact that she had been trying to add to her mother's agony, made her feel sick about herself. On that the following night, she just sneaked into her mom's room and slept hugging her. Susanne head her sobbing but did not say anything. She knew it was a time for silence instead of any dialogues between them. Susanne huged Richa back and they finally slept after crying for a long time. Richa was in shock after her father's sudden death. She felt left out when her mother cared for her brothers after coming back from the office. By provoking her brothers, she wanted to make her presence felt and wanted to gain attention from her mom. That was not intentional but was the unconscious behavior of a Teenager.

That night Susanne slept peacefully after a long time. The next morning when Susanne woke up, she did not find Richa. When she walked into the living room, she found Richa all dressed up for her college. She had made breakfast for all four of them and had woken up her brothers and got them to have their breakfast. Seeing her Mom, she rushed to her, gave a kiss on her cheeks, wished her Good morning and went to college after hugging her little brothers and waving them a goodbye with a sweet smile. All that Susanne did was watching her kids bond with each other after a very long time. With great relief, she smiled to herself and got back to the kitchen to pack lunch for the kids.

Patience

Teenagers test our patience like no one else in this world. They are convinced most of the time that they know it all and you look like an idiot in front of them. So, even though you are losing your call or finding it difficult to control your emotions, you have to behave like an adult. Try to listen more and react less. Try not to take things personally. Everything that they do or say is a decision taken at the spur of the moment. Most of the time, they do not even mean to say it. So, behave in a matured way and try to take control of the situation. Avoid any melodrama being created at home, spoiling the mood of the entire family.

Step back into the past when you were a Teenager. We, as a Teenager, also had our own struggles and challenged our parents in many ways. Those days were not easy for them and so are these days for us. Overreacting and losing patience are going to put all our efforts to an end. We should try to understand that they are no longer under our control. They have their own wings now and are getting ready to fly soon. It is ok if they break some basic rules of tidying up their room, helping you at home, getting the best grades, treating their siblings with compassion. There are many challenging battles in life, which you want them to get prepared for. Therefore, if they are missing smaller ones keep calm and let it pass. They will slowly learn and understand why you mean something.

I always felt my mother had very little patience when I was a Teenager. However, I soon realized my perception was wrong. She is one of the most patient women I have ever known. Maybe I was too early to judge her. We are best friends now and she inspires me to be patient with my Teenager. This is how the Teenage years are. All we need to do is hold on there and let things pass. Things are going to be better soon.

Conversation

Ali has always been an inquisitive kid from his childhood. Growing up into a Teenager made him questioning more regarding anything and everything. His curiosity knew no bounds. As a child, he wanted to know what the cost of everything is, how old is everyone, etc. His Dad, Faiz, was a Chartered Accountant and managed accounts of some really well-to-do businesspersons.

One night after dinner, when his Dad was busy in his library, working on his accounts, Ali barged in and sat next to him. Confused, his dad asked him what he wanted. Usually, the family never disturbed him when he was at work. Ali said he was getting bored so he thought of coming and helping his dad. Faiz said that he would not be able to allow him to share his work as it was a bit complicated and Ali will never be able to understand. Following is their conversation.

Ali: *"Abbu (Dad), I know it is all about accounts, but I am a grown-up boy now and my major is Accounts in my school. So, you can share stuff with me."*

Faiz: *"Ok, glad to know you understand, tell me what you want to know."*

Ali: *"I am not interested in knowing about other's accounts. If you don't mind, can you tell me how much you charge for each client of yours?"*

(Faiz did not know how to handle this question. Until today neither his parents, brothers nor his wife questioned

him about this. He initially hesitated and was not sure if he should really take the conversation forward. Then he remembered what one of his clients – a renowned Psychologist had told him lately – "Be transparent with your Teenager.")

Faiz: *"I will tell you. But what would you do with this information?"*

Ali: *"I just want to know how much you earn in a month that you slog so much even after coming home."*

Faiz: *(smiling) "Ok, so you want to know how much I earn…amount a month."*

Ali: *"Abbu, then how do you manage everything that you are doing now? You know Daadi (Grandma) has a caretaker at home. You help out Ammi(Mom) in her business, you send money to Aapa (elder sister) for her M.D. And even my Football coaching is very costly."*

(Ali started putting on paper all the monthly expenses and was making calculations)

Faiz: *"Don't bother about all that stuff. You concentrate on your studies and get admission in a good college. That would make me happy."*

Ali: *"Abbu, I always thought you earned more than …. and so are able to manage everything that we ask for. I am sorry to have bothered you to spend money on my Football coaching too. That must have been a real burden for you."*

Faiz: *"That's ok, you can't always sit studying. You need some break to relieve your stress. So, Football is a necessity and not a burden."*

Ali: *"Thank you so much Abbu. I wish I could become a person like you, who does not complaint in spite of doing so much for the family. I promise you I will get admission in a good college. I want to apply for an education loan instead of burdening you more for my education. You should have ideally done that for Aapa too. Things would have been much easier to manage in that case. I will not do that mistake."*

(Faiz understood the importance of sharing stuff with kids. Being a CA, even he did not think of taking an education loan for his daughter. How could he miss that! Ali had not been an easy Teenager to handle because of his temper and tantrums. Nevertheless, this incident proved, that irrespective of the experiences, you need to have an open dialogue with your kids. Who knows, there might be some good learning from them too.)

Transparency

Do not hide things from your Teens. Their brains are slowly maturing and they can comprehend what you are trying to tell them. Involve them in your decisions, explain the situation, tell them the choices and the consequences of each situation. Even if you are trying to impose some restrictions on them, let them know why you are doing it. Do not worry about what their reactions or feelings would be. Even if they get it wrong the first few times, they will slowly start understanding the importance of transparency in their future relations.

Being honest can be quite difficult for some people, especially when you are confronted by your Teenager who asks questions about everything. By being honest and open with your child, you are allowing them to retain the necessary information they need to have to be able to make the right choice. They will be able to decide more and more for themselves, which shows strong character and confidence. In addition, this will form a strong base for positive mental health as well.

Parents should talk to their Teens about family values and beliefs around money during their formative years — in an age-appropriate way. The lifestyle your kids enjoy now is based on *your* financial success and may not be the lifestyle they will be able to achieve when they leave the nest. They need to be prepared for what could be a big lifestyle change as they head out on their own. Helping them understand the importance of work and directing them on a path toward meaningful, useful employment is critical to their long-term happiness, and yours too. Your Teens should know they will have to work, both to earn money to support themselves and to find the purpose and enjoyment in using their gifts and talents.

Incident

Suman lived in a joint family with her parents, grandparents and uncle's family. Her dad and uncle managed a grocery business and were busy all the time. She had two siblings and two cousins who were younger to her. Her mom and aunt were homemakers and were busy all the time taking care of the younger kids and the elders at home. Suman helped her mom a lot in the household chores, played with the younger one and took great care of her grandparents. Unfortunately, everybody in the house was so busy, that they hardly acknowledged Suman's helping nature. She was in her Xth grade and managed to get good marks at school. None at home enquired about her studies, her school or friends. She had no friends around her neighborhood to spend time with and was slowly becoming more silent and subdued.

Her aunt, Sushila, visited during one of the festivals with her family. They lived in a distant city. Sushila's daughter Naini, was studying in seventh grade and was excited to meet Suman. Nevertheless, Suman could not reciprocate well. She continued doing her regular chores but suddenly stopped being happy. Sushila was shocked to see such a bubbly girl suddenly going silent. One evening, when the kids went out to the nearest exhibition, Sushila had a quick chat with the family. She asked them about the reason for Suman's changed behavior. None had observed this until then. Her old grandma who was ill finally spoke about how

Suman was always helping the family, sometimes helping her uncle and dad in the grocery store, and taking care of them. But no one bothered to appreciate her efforts. While kids of her age were happy going to some hobby classes, she was at home taking care of her brothers and cousins. She said that the family never bothered to appreciate her contribution.

Sushila was upset upon hearing all this. She went inside the house and came out with Suman's bag. She asked her family if they were aware that Suman got an appreciation letter from her school principal. Suman also received a scholarship for her XIth grade owing to her performance this year. They nodded their head and denied. Tears rolled down Sushila's eyes realizing that Suman never shared this with her family.

Everyone realized their mistake and felt guilty for their behavior towards Suman. The family decided to correct themselves and Sushila suggested a great idea. By the time, the kids returned home, they were shocked to see the house decorated with lights. There was a party going on. Suman was surprised to see her neighbors, relatives, her teachers along with Principal present at her house. Everyone was waiting for Suman to return. In front of everyone, her Principal handed over the appreciation letter and the Scholarship award. Her parents apologize for not appreciating all that she did. Suman burst out crying and hugged her parents. Her parents told her how proud they were. Everyone had a great time at the party.

Following that day, everything that Suman did got appreciation from her family. She got rewarded in the form of kind words, hugs and gifts. Suman regained her bubbly nature and was now a much more confident girl. She topped the District Board in her XIIth. She received a scholarship for her Engineering in a reputed college of India.

Appreciation

Appreciate your Teens for what they are and do it as often as possible. Appreciation builds self-confidence and morale. Teenagers look for a lot of validation and the appreciation received satisfies this craving. It also helps in the long run when they face failure in life and in their self-esteem dips down. Always reward them when they do something good, irrespective of how bad they have been in the past. Carrying the experiences, incidents in the mind is not the right thing to do. Celebrate their small victories. Do not lose a chance of appreciating them in front of everyone. There is a difference between appreciating and boasting. Boasting results in overconfidence but appreciation helps build self-esteem.

Too often, the assumption is made that a Teenager knows how much they are loved and valued as a member of the family, but this may not be the case. As we rush through our responsibilities each day and often look to our Teenagers for help with chores around the house, making meals, and looking after younger siblings, it is important to make a conscious effort to thank the Teen in an honest manner. Adding physical indications of appreciation and affection from your Teenager can further enhance this positivity. When away from home, verbal praise can be accompanied by simple touch – a stroke on the arm, a pat on the back or a quick arm around the shoulders is enough to get the message across. At home, where Teens are more comfortable and less concerned, full hugs could be given.

Demonstrating appreciation and affection for your Teen and their efforts will improve their outlook with regard to both their place in the family and their value outside of the home. It is a simple act but can make a lot of difference.

Conversation

Mom: *How was your day at school?*

Simona: *Fine, how about yours?*

Mom: *Mine was good. I got some time to relax between my training sessions.*

(Avoid -> Mom: *"Mine was good too."* **If this is all that the parent says, the conversation can easily end here.)**

Simona: *That is good to hear.*

Mom: *Do you sometimes feel like there are too many things on your plate and you feel like chilling a bit, like I felt today.*

Simona: *Yep…like now.*

Mom: *Yeah…really?*

(Avoid -> Mom: *"Why now? What is going on? Can I do anything to help?"*

These questions can feel intrusive to the Teenager at this point, leading to possible shut down in communication.)

Simona: *There is so much to do. The projects, tests, papers, homework, you know, the usual.*

Mom: *That sounds like a lot of work.*

(Avoid -> Mom: *"That's nothing. If you can't handle that, how will you be able to handle real life?"* **These comments minimize and deny the Teenager's experiences.)**

Simona: Yes, it is. Everything is due this week. I do not understand why teachers cannot spread out the deadlines. They try to rush and it really gets difficult.

Mom: That would be easier, is it?

Simona: Yes, it would help when each thing had a different deadline.

Mom: So, what is your plan?

(Avoid -> Mom: *"You need to learn to deal with this better. Life does not work the way you want it to. If you had listened to me and planned things better, you would not be in this mess now."* **While what the parent says may be true but she no longer has a conversation partner now.)**

Simona: I guess, I need to take one step at a time.

Mom: That sounds like a smart strategy. Please let me know if I can be of some help.

(Avoid -> Mom: *"That's not enough. You need to have a more detailed plan. That is what I do at work too. You have seen me handling so many stuff simultaneously …..blah… blah…"* **If your Teen was not stressed so far, she/he will get stressed now, having had this frustrating, unhelpful, disconnecting conversation with the parent.)**

Simona: Sure, Thanks Mom.

Communication

This is one of the critical ingredients of the filling. If this is not present, then you will never get to know what is going on in your Teen's life. Do not neglect their silence. You do not have to be in advice mode when you talk to them. Instead, keep them engaged in topics they like. This way the communication channel is always open. When the Teens feel comfortable talking to you, they will also end up expressing their issues, fears and feelings. Most of the suicides that happen in Teenage years are due to lack of this ingredient in parenting. When the Teen feels there is no one they can share their feelings with, they suddenly feel low and take any drastic step. So, please...........keep your communication channel open and make conscious efforts to allow the Teen to express whatever they feel like.

To communicate with your child, you need to make yourself available. Young adolescents resist "scheduled" talks; they don't open up when you tell them to, but when they want to. Some Teens like to talk when they first get home from school. Others may like to talk at the dinner table or at bedtime. Some parents talk with their children in the car, preferably when the radio, tapes and CDs are not playing. Responding too strongly can lead to yelling and screaming and it can shut down the conversation. Try to keep anxiety and emotions out of the conversation— then they will open up.

Communication breaks down for some parents because they find it hard to manage differences with their children. Differences of opinion are easier to manage when we recognize that these differences can provide important opportunities for us to rethink the limits and to negotiate new ones, a skill that is valuable for your child to develop. The key, according to psychologists, is to be inquisitive but not interfering, working to respect your child's privacy as you establish trust and closeness.

Incident

Ritvik returns from college and walks away into his room angrily. His parents understand he is upset over something that happened at college. His mom goes to ask him something but he shuts the door on her face. His mom is terribly upset and complains to her husband that these days he hardly shares stuff with her. Later in the evening, he comes out to watch TV and sits in the living room. His mom comes there with his favorite snack plate and enquires on what happened in the college. He shares that he and two of his friends got punished by the Principal. They got suspended from the college for the entire week. Listening to this, his mom starts questioning about what they did. She also starts cribbing about the behavior of the current generation of boys, etc. Also about the management taking stern decisions against the students without bothering about their future. She goes on.

Ritvik's father intervenes, tells her he would continue talking to him, and asks her to go and finish her cooking. He assures her that he will handle the situation. He starts a friendly conversation with Ritvik and finds out the actual reason for suspension. He learns that one of Ritvik's school friends needed blood for an emergency operation. Since there were study hours in the afternoon session, instead of informing the Principal and taking permission they sneaked out and went to the hospital. While returning to the college, they were caught by their Principal and without listening to the reason, the Principal decided to suspend them. Ritvik's father understood the situation. Instead of advising Ritvik, he empathized with him but also made him understand the Principal's perspective. Ritvik agreed. Then his father shares an incident during his college days where he had to face something similar. They both have a good laugh. At the same time, Ritvik's mom is fuming watching them from the kitchen. Ritvik always openly shares stuff with his father instead of his mother. This is because his mom would always jump to conclusions or offer help or try to fix things for him, which he hates. She never tries to learn or understand his side of the story.

Open Mind

Non-judgmental attitude of the parent helps the Teenager connect better with the parent and share things. Most of us tend to pass our judgments, as soon as the kids share something with us. Relax, allow them to speak, try to put yourself in their shoe and then give your opinion. Teenager's perspective is very different from ours. The earlier we buy this fact, the better. They have a different way of looking at things. So, before coming to any conclusions, give some time to think what made them say something, or, what made them do something. If you are in confusion, get clarification by questioning them in a casual manner. An open mind and open heart are really required to be able to accept your Teen the way they are.

Being open-minded means that someone accepts the fact that other people can and will act according to their wish and not yours. Every Teenager has a different vision of how his or her life should be. Some Teens look at success and money as an achievement. Some others look at academics and good grades. Some Teens are mentally strong, have better clarity in life, motivated all the time and can set and move towards their goals. Some are lazy, want to relax and take it easy. Rest of them lie somewhere in between the two kinds, they are ready to get pushed and achieve results.

Parents who strive to be open-minded try to understand the other side of the story. By asking relevant questions, they try to understand other's opinions. They know that differences exist and they are neither worse nor better, just different with all shades. Take advantage of teachable moments. Use everyday events in your life to point out things you like your Teen to know about. Point out regarding the ill-effects of using alcohol and drugs, take opportunity of discussing about infatuation and consequences related to sex and wrong decisions. Check if they have got the information right. For a more engaging conversation, ask questions that are more open-ended.

Incident

Rahul as a child always wanted to be a doctor. His first attempt in the Medicine entrance does not fetch him a government seat. He does not want his parents to pay a huge amount to get a seat through management quota. Therefore, he decides to take a long-term coaching for a year and re-appear for the Medicine exam. His parents get worried that he would be losing a year in comparison with his friends. However, Rahul is not ready to take up graduation in any of the other science streams. He is very keen to pursue his medicine. His parents agree and enroll him in a long-term coaching for his medicine exam. All through the year, Rahul puts in his best effort.

Due to some political reasons, at the year-end, the medicine entrance exam gets postponed. Admissions in other colleges, for paid seats, start being filled up. Rahul's parents start panicking. They are unable to decide whether to wait for him to give the exam and the results to come out. They get worried that in case he does not get a good rank this time; he might lose another year and might have to join the Bachelor in Sciences. Therefore, without his knowledge, they try to block a paid seat in a Medical college by paying some advance amount. When Rahul comes to know about this, he gets upset. He questions his parents why they had no confidence in him. Instead of encouraging him, they were trying to play safe. His parents realize his seriousness and commitment towards the goal that he had set for himself.

With the encouragement of his parents and family, Rahul secures a good rank in the entrance examination and gets admission in one of the best government medical colleges in the city. His parents and family feel proud of him. His friends and relatives also appreciate his decision of opting for a long-term coaching instead of just taking admission into some bachelor's graduation as they did.

Encouragement

Always help your Teenager to dream big. As parents, we have a lot of apprehensions and doubts regarding our Teenager's capabilities and potential. However, never express those fears. Always act positive and encouraging them to move ahead and set high goals in life. Any Teen with the lowest confidence levels will turn around and do big with constant encouragement. Do not pressurize them, encouragement is a positive attitude, pressurizing is a negative trait. Try to understand the subtle difference, help them excel and be ready to face any situation in life – be it Success or Failure.

Acknowledging and accepting the things your Teen wants to pursue is a switch that turns on their brain activity. It fires their imagination, stimulates creativity and opens the door to a world of opportunities. Many Teenagers feel that they are yet to conclude on a specific dream or goal for the future. Nevertheless, you do not have to wait to get started. One of the simplest – and most effective – ways to help Teens is to encourage them to try a wide variety of activities. Please be ready with a 'Yes' when they want to try out a new activity or take the next step in pursuing their interest. Remember that your 'Yes', will mean a commitment of your time, energy and money. However, you are paving a way for them to try out stuff and decide for themselves. Some of these efforts might not go well but that is fine. At least they are getting a chance to look at all the options that they have, try them out and get convinced what they are not good at. At every juncture, be with them and let them know that it does not matter whether they succeed or fail. Teach them how to handle failure.

Encouragement is the best way to motivate or inspire your Teenager. Constant encouragement has created miracles in the lives of Teenagers who have given up on their life goals, ambitions fearing failure, some even tried to take their lives. Respect them as individuals and not as people who need to excel in every area of life.

Incident

Akhil and Nikhil were twins. While Akhil was an extrovert, his brother Nikhil was an introvert and liked to be by himself. He was the target of his parents as well as the teachers as they all failed to understand that they were both two different individuals. He felt a lot of pressure due to the expectations being set on him. He had his own talents and skills but people failed to notice. He loved art and liked writing poetry. While Akhil was busy excelling at academics and sports, Nikhil captured the entire world around him in the form of drawings and poems. Since he knew his parents would not appreciate all this, he hid his diary and paintings.

In their Xth board exams, Akhil scored 97% while Nikhil scored only 82%. Their parents were upset with Nikhil and embarrassed him in front of all his relatives. Every person has something called a Defining moment in his or her life. These can create either a positive or negative impact and affect the person's self-belief. The incident where his parents offended him in front of everyone came as a shock to Nikhil and he went into depression. While Akhil went ahead and got admission into a top engineering institute, Nikhil was at home attending counselling sessions for his depression. The counsellor suggested a personal coach for Nikhil. The coach spent time with Nikhil and got to learn more about his values, belief system and his defining moments. He discussed them with his parents and made them realize what they did wrong during their parenting.

Nikhil opened up to the coach as a friend. In the process, he also shared his paintings and poetry with him. The coach recognized his talent and stook the help of a friend, a book publisher, to convert them into a book for children. Nikhil became the youngest author of the city and started getting media attention. His life totally took a 180-degree turn and he suddenly became famous. He started writing regularly for a famous newspaper and magazine. On the suggestion of his coach, his parents agreed for him to pursue his graduation in Literature instead of the main streams.

Understanding

Know your Teen (KYT) is a Tool that I share with the parents in my program. Most of the time, as a parent, we neglect to check if we really know our child in and out. Awareness brings understanding and understanding helps us set expectations about our child. We always try to compare our Teen with the Teen next door. However, have we tried to understand that the two kids in the above incident are very different from each other? Every child is different and unique. We should encourage them to do what they are good at. If they do not perform well in other areas, which is not their strength, you should understand enough to let it be. Do not force them to do things they do not like.

The first step to understanding your Teen is to ask questions, but be strategic about it. Many Teens give yes or no answers when you ask them a question. The trick is to engage them when they are more likely to open up, such as when they are not with friends or running around. Driving in the car seems to be a good time, assuming that they do not have headphones on. When you ask questions, make sure to listen to the answers even if you do not understand half of the words they are using. It is okay to ask for clarification. As you are listening, take mental notes. One of the other ways to understand your Teen is to "listen in" their conversations. True, most of their conversations are via text message so "listening in" is not exactly an option, but you can snag their cell phone from time to time and read their text messages. If this feels too invasive, try to be around them when they are with their friends. Encourage them to invite their friends over, volunteer to drive them to places, and invite them along to events or activities. Get to know your Teenager when they are around with their friends.

Each generation has its own trends, language, and interests. It is normal and totally okay not to completely relate with your Teenager. Do what you can to connect with them. Let them know that you are interested in their lives and then relax.

Incident

Krupa was a very obedient and sincere girl. From her childhood, she had a good company of friends at school, who were also her friends from the same residential society. She studied in a girls school since childhood but her Dad got transferred to a new city and she had to move to a co-ed school for her higher classes. She never interacted much with boys earlier to this. Therefore, when she saw the new atmosphere around her, she was totally lost. She did not know how to react. Her mom, Ranjana, had advised her to stay away from the boys, as she was not used to handling them earlier. She also gave Krupa, a set of rules to follow at school.

The first few days, she just followed what her Mom said but as days passed by, she started observing the groups of students around her. She found a group of girls and boys who were supposed to be a part of the coolest group of high school. One of the boys from that group would always keep looking at her when she passed by them. She ignored this for 1-2 days. After that, one of the girls from that group approached Krupa and made friends with her. She insisted Krupa to join that group and Krupa accepted. She enjoyed being a part of the group. She tried to fit in by making a lot of changes to herself. She enjoyed the attention she was getting but did not understand most of the stuff they were discussing. After a few months, when Krupa got comfortable with the group, she started lying to her Mom. She would go out with the group giving the excuse of doing a combined study. They even started bunking school and watching movies.

One day, when Ranjana was shopping with her friend in a mall, she saw Krupa and her friends entering the multiplex to watch a movie. She was surprised to see Krupa in a very different attire and full of make-up. She just could not believe her eyes. Her friend also observed this and asked her to go and question Krupa at that very moment. However, Ranjana thought for a while and decided to rather take the other way round. Ranjana's friend got aggressive and started bad-mouthing about Teenagers. She insisted Ranjana to call her husband right away and inform him about what happened. However, Ranjana asked her to relax. She told her friend that she would like to handle it in her own way. Had she informed her husband at that time,, the situation might have got worse and that was not what she wanted to happen. She went back home and waited for Krupa to return.

Krupa came back home in her school uniform with her hair tied back with ribbons. Ranjana behaved as if nothing had happened. After a while, Ranjana walked to Krupa's room and asked her to try out a dress, which she purchased for her from the mall that day. Krupa liked the dress and asked her the name of the mall. When Ranjana uttered the name if the mall, Krupa got shocked. Ranjana told her that she also wanted to watch a movie with her friend but decided against it. Krupa started to sweat. As Ranjana was about to leave the room she turned back immediately and told Krupa that she saw a girl who looked exactly like Krupa. She continued that her friend confused that girl for Krupa and tried to call her. However, Ranjana was sure it was not their Krupa because Krupa has never lied to mother since her childhood.

Krupa burst out and tears rolled out of her eyes. She understood that her mother actually knew it was her, but was just waiting to hear from her. Ranjana cajoled her and hugged her. Krupa narrateed the entire story to Ranjana; how she longed for attention from that group and wanted to be part of it. She apologized for lying and plead her not to tell to her dad. Ranjana pacified her and told her to relax. After Krupa calmed down, Ranjana narrated a few incidents that happened in the city recently because of the careless attitude of the Teenagers. She made her understand the consequences of some wrong decisions taken. Krupa realized that her Mom was like a friend and was finally relieved after sharing the past instances with her. From the next day onward, Krupa refused to go out of the school whenever the group insisted. The group slowly started ignoring Krupa and now Krupa is back to her normal self and concentrating on her studies as she used to earlier.

Friendship (Vs Parenting)

Many people turn a deaf ear to the fact that you can become your Teenager's friend. Therefore, this ingredient needs to be included very cautiously and only in specific situations. If you feel you can never befriend your Teen monster, you can decide to skip this ingredient or add bit by bit and see how it tastes.

Do not act like a parent 100% of the time. Try to be a friend sometimes. In an interview, I was asked, if I treat my Teenager with love or friendship. Love makes us protect our child from all the mishaps in their life. This can spare us a lot of anxiety. However, keeping the Teens in the safe zone all the time hinders their mental development. Friends challenge each other, share stuff that is close to their heart, fight, patch up and make a relation for a lifetime. Behaving like a friend instead of a parent helps them get much closer to you.

I agree that this might not work in situations where you need to make a decision as a parent for their safety and security. In such a scenario, you might have to switch the roles. However, if you want them to have open communication with you, it is required for you to be a friendly parent. Therefore, not losing the authoritative role, but still trying to respond, how a friend does in situations, is required in cases of many Teenagers.

When it comes to making decisions or taking up responsibilities, you might have to discuss like a friend to come up with a common understanding between both of you. Ordering like a parent does not work out in these situations. When you discuss like a friend, they are more open to have a conversation and ready to own up their responsibilities or roles.

Incident

Natasha was in her IXth grade, studying in an International school. She was a bright student at school and was a member of the local charity club. She met students from other schools during the events of charity. Sometimes she had to stay away from home during her camps of charity. Since Natasha's parents were very confident about their upbringing and values, they allowed her to do so. They liked encouraging her to do what she liked. During summer, Natasha signed up for a weekend camp in a nearby village. Students from different international schools also signed up for the same.

Natasha's dad droped her off at the camp and picked her up after three days. They got back to a regular routine but after a few days, her parents start observing a change in Natasha's behavior. She started getting more aggressive and prefered spending most of the time in her room. Her parents started getting worried. They followed her to her school and back home without being noticed. One day, her dad got shocked to see her not taking her usual school route. He followed her and later found her bicycle parked in front of a big bungalow in a posh locality in the city. Carefully, he sneaked into the compound. He found the door locked from inside and heard laughter from inside. When he peeped through the window, he found Natasha with two other girls and four boys. On close observation, he saw that the boys were taking drugs and alcohol. They encouraged the girls to do the same. He saw that one of the guys was forcibly trying to get closer to another girl in the group. Natasha's father saw the girl objecting, but that wouldn't stop the guy. Natasha keps saying 'No' but then gave in to take the drugs. When she was about to sniff the drug powder, Natasha's father broke the window glass and the kids got alerted. The four boys fleeted away and Natasha was shocked to see her father there. He broke into the house.

Natasha's dad droped all the girls to their houses and shared what he saw with their parents. Most of the parents ended up beating them, punishing them or threatening them. Natasha silently walked into her house and when her mom questioned her, she started shivering and broke down. She confessed that she met a new group of friends during the camp. They carried drugs with them and forced her to take it. She did not want to do it, but during the camp, she had to give in to their pressure. Instead of scolding her or punishing her, Natasha's dad apologized to her and said that it was his mistake not to warn her of this stuff before he allowed sending her to outside camps.

Her parents cajoled her and gave her some time to get out of this experience. They all went out for a trekking vacation. During the trip, they shared some examples of the consequences of such bad addiction. They also shared the story of their distant relative who was in a juvenile house due to his erratic behavior after taking drugs and alcohol. Natasha understood the dangers of such addictions; and how it influenced the Teenagers and their families too. She thanked her parents for their understanding and promised to keep away from that group of new friends. She got back to her regular school. With the help of her parents, she convinced her school management to conduct a weekly class on Life skills and education on these topics so that the other students do not fall prey to such undue pressure and get into addiction.

Education on Sex/Alcohol/Drugs/Abuse

If you were just wondering, why I would mention it as an ingredient of parenting, think about all the things that might go wrong if you do not inform your Teen about what is right. It is better for Teens to get the right information from their parents or teachers rather than being misinformed from other sources like magazines, friends, internet. It is really an awkward situation and not an easy conversation to start. Do not wait for a perfect time to start the discussion. You might miss the opportunities then. In addition, before you begin, you would like to discuss it with your partner and decide upon your approach.

Sex education is a parent's responsibility. Think of sex education as an ongoing conversation between you and your Teenager. If there is a chance to discuss it, take the plunge. When you watch something on the internet or TV related to ethics or issues related to sexual behavior, use it as a beginning point for your discussion. It is easy to take advantage of everyday moments like shopping together, riding in the car when you get time to spending with your Teenager alone. If either they or you feel uncomfortable, acknowledge that but let them know that you need to continue the conversation. If you do not know how to answer their questions, look up but answer their questions. Do not try to lecture them or scare them with the consequences, instead, present the risks that are involved, the emotional stress, sexually transmitted diseases, unplanned pregnancies, etc. Create the pain and show them the life where they do not have to deal with any of these uncalled for situations and enjoy a jolly and happy life as a Teenager focusing on stuff they really want to.

Closely observe their reactions when you are doing all the above. Some Teens are much more educated about this even before you start the discussion. Some feel embarrassed to hear such stuff from their parents. You, as a parent, can decide how much to talk about and when. You can plug in points about feelings, attitude and values to make it connected. You can also pitch in ethics and responsibility in the context of your family values or religious beliefs. Your Teen can emerge as a sexually responsible adult only with your support. Be honest and speak right from the heart. Keep in mind that this may be the only time your Teen will ever talk about sexuality in an honest way. Some of them would act disinterested, but you go ahead and say it. He or she will probably be listening. They might not be willing to listen or question now. So, end your conversation by inviting them to more discussion when they feel like. Inform them that they can approach you anytime they want to talk to you about it or when they have any questions and concerns. If they happen to approach you with any questions later, do not react. Instead, appreciate them first and then start the discussion.

Alcohol and drug use continues to be a significant global problem with many health and economic consequences.

Multiple studies have shown that the majority of adults who end up with an alcohol/drug use disorder have their first contact with these substances as adolescents. The pressure to experiment with these substances can come from friends and peers. If you suspect your child is using these substances, open a discussion about the dangers involved with using tobacco, alcohol, and drugs. If you or someone else in the household smokes, now is a good time to quit. Watching a parent struggle through the process of quitting can be a powerful message for a Teen who is thinking about starting. It also shows that you care about your health, as well as your Teens'.

The main reasons why a teen gets into this trap is

- social circle and peer pressure

- escape unhappiness

- beating boredom

- show their rebellious behavior

- lack of self-esteem and self-confidence

- misinformation

- considering it as a status symbol

Most of the time, parents have a chance to catch them early, if they are observant. Try to help your adolescent build their self-confidence or self-esteem. Frequently ask them about any concerns and problems they are facing and help them learn how to deal with strong emotions and cope with stress in ways that are healthy. For instance, encourage them to participate in leisure and outside activities with Teens who do not drink and take drugs. Discuss examples of the consequences of wrong decisions and unhealthy habits whenever you come across any. The more open you are about these topics, the more you get to discuss with them, you can put across your opinions and warn them.

Incident

Samuel and his wife Irina were teachers at a high school. They had twin daughters who were now entering into their Teens. While most of the parents struggled with just one Teenager at home, Sam and Irina were comfortably able to parent their Teens. The teachers handling Teenagers every day at school taught them many things. They were better prepared to handle their daughters at home. Each one would take up the role of a parent in turns. In times of conflict between their girls, they would also take sides of both of them.

One day, their girls were having a conversation about a new announcement at school about the volunteering activity. Irina overheard the conversation but did not get involved. The conversation turned into an argument and she understood it was time for her to intervene.

Conversation

Irina: *"May I know what is your discussion all about."*

Rinky: *"Mom, there was an announcement at school about volunteering for Blood donation camp this weekend at our school campus."*

Irina: *"So, what's about it?"*

Pinky: *"Rinky and I have our Tennis tournament. Rinky is my partner for Doubles and she wants to go to the Blood donation camp instead of coming for the tournament."*

Irina: "Hmm... I get it now."

Sam (entering into the living room):

"Hey, the three beautiful women of my house seem to be having good chitchat without me. Are you planning for a secret weekend outing without me?"

Rinky: "Come on Dad, you always cannot try to be funny. Please be serious sometimes. Pinky is not agreeing to my volunteering for the Blood donation camp this weekend."

Pinky: "Oh, come on! You promised to be my partner for the Tennis doubles tournament and you are backing out. How stupid can that be!"

Rinky: "I never wanted to be part of it, you insisted. Now it is my turn to make a decision and I want to do what I like."

(Sam and Irina looked at each other and smiled)

Sam: "Well, that sounds like a major situation to handle. Let us do something. Instead of arguing, both of you go into your rooms, sit with yourselves for 15 minutes, and come back here. Both of you come up with options for how to handle this. What are your thoughts on this?"

(Both of them nod in agreement and walked towards their rooms. After 15 minutes, they assembled back in their living room, with a much calmer and peaceful look on their faces)

Sam: "So, Rinky what's your option?"

Rinky: "The Blood donation camp is for the entire day but the tournament is only in the first half of the day. I *can participate in the tournament along with Pinky in the morning and take permission from my Principal to join the camp after I am done with the tournament. Either Mom or you might have to drive me to my school from the tournament."*

Irina: *"What's your option Pinky?"*

Pinky: *"If Rinky agrees to support me in the tournament, I would love to accompany her back and also be a volunteer for the Blood donation camp."*

Sam: *"That sounds like a plan then. Problem sorted!"*

(Sam winked at Irina and they watched both the sisters walking away hand in hand)

Empowerment

The best way to empower any person is by asking them the right questions. This is how I was empowered by my daughter to take up my passion. Though your Teen will not have the answers right away, you have done the job of planting the seed in their mind and it will do its part. This question will keep pondering in their mind repeatedly and they will get into a self-evaluation mode. Triggering self-evaluation is better than advising. All the great coaches and mentors in this world use this technique to bring transformation in people and is a proven one. Empower your children to discover their strengths, their weaknesses, take up challenges and set some goals in their life.

Empowering our Teenagers is to teach them to take charge of their own life by giving them some basic directions. For most Teens, this does not come naturally. They learn it through experiences. Their intellects and reasoning are unquestionable. They care deeply for the things they like. Still, they need a small lift from our side to make them understand their interest areas. Some of the Teenagers like volunteering for some social activities, others like to be part of motivational groups. Their interests could be many and it is our duty to encourage them to take up activities that they are good at. Discuss all the possibilities, choices available and consequences of each choice they make. They need to be aware that if they are spending time on the activities that they are interested in, they will also be responsible to manage other schoolwork, assignments and projects in a timely manner. With a sense of responsibility comes commitment and the zeal to push themselves beyond their comfort level.

Ask them the right questions on their vision, mission and goals in their life. Do not ridicule them when these do not fall in line with your expectations or plans for your Teenager. After all, it is their life and you are just a medium to unleash the best potential in them.

Incident

While my daughter Prerana is my inspiration to take up my passion, the first people to inspire me were my parents. My Dad started a school close to my home and named it 'Praveen Vidyaniketan'. Since he was a full-time Public sector employee, he made my mother the Headmistress of the school. The school started as a small pre-school and slowly developed into a high school. I really do not remember a lot about my challenges as a Teenager because all during this time, I saw my parents busy trying to help others. My mom was a hard-working person and had dawned on to the role of a Headmistress from a homemaker. My Dad would help in terms of planning and organizing while my mom would handle all the operations.

I would watch a lot of students' parents coming up to my parents and discussing their problems. My parents would offer them help. All of a sudden, our mediocre life turned into a life of contribution to the society. All our neighbors and relatives treated my parents with great respect. As their only child, I really got inspired watching what they were doing. Even though I tried to come up with some Teenage tantrums, I realized there was no time for it in our lives. I would help my mom give tuitions to the kids after school. We led a very simple life but that with a purpose. A lot of stuff that I am seeing these days in many families was never part of our life. My Teenage years just flew by. I wanted to make my parents proud one day and so did not have to get instructed by them to do good in my academics. I would try to finish my studies as quickly as possible so that I could, in some way, help in the schoolwork. This helped me get self-motivated. They never instructed me to do what they wanted. Instead, they indirectly inspired me through their own lives, one step at a time. I decided that there was no way I could let them down and the result was that I got into one of the prestigious institutes in India, BITS, Pilani, for my graduation.

To this day, I feel proud to be their daughter, when I see their students come down to meet them and share their success stories.

Inspiration

According to me, the best way to inspire your Teen is to become a role model for them. If you have not done things that you always wanted to do, or you gave up on your dreams, your passion, you have never respected your family, elders, never contributed to the society; then it is high time you bring those changes in yourself. Your Teen is watching you and very closely. If you really want them to be great human beings, you have to be one.

Before moaning and groaning about your Teenager, please have a close look at yourself. If you expect that they need to get inspired and motivated in different areas of their life, the first thing, which you need to do, is to check yourself out. Do you have the aura around you, which can inspire them? Sometimes, parents might not be able to create self-examples. Due to various reasons, they might not be able to become role models themselves. In such a scenario, create an ambience at home that inspires them. Discuss about people who are doing great in their lives. It could be any area of life. Show examples of people who are self-made, who have bounced back in their life after many failures, who have reached great heights after a shift in their attitude. Do not try to advise or instruct them to follow. Just try to bring up examples as part of the regular discussions. These are nothing but giving them life lessons. A Teenager who is strong in Life skills can handle any biggest roadblocks in life.

Most of us parents think that only academics and securing a job are the most important goals for a Teenager. However, that is not the case. What's the use of a distinction which does not teach your Teenager to face any untoward failures in their life.

Incident

Gaurav had a terrible fight with his Mom after coming late from his friend's house after a party. Both of them were so angry that they didn't speak to each other the next morning. Gaurav's mother was a short-tempered woman and could never control her emotions. It was never possible for her to respond instead of reacting. Gaurav was their only child and so she was optimistic of discipline and obedience from him. Gaurav's Dad was a neutral man with a good sense of humor and tried to lighten up the environment at home whenever there was a conflict. He tried to speak to both his wife and son asking them to let it be and move on. However, things seemed to be getting worse. Dinner table became a difficult place for both Gaurav and his Mom to face each other.

That night, Gaurav's Dad decided to do something about it. He got an idea. He was on the internet where found what he wanted. He quickly printed something for his wife and his son and stuck it at the mirrors in their respective bedrooms.

Note for his wife read:

Parents with Teenagers know exactly why animals eat their young ones.

> *"You can learn many things from your children.*
> *How much patience you have for instance."*

—Franklin P. Jones

How Mean Moms are born:

Teen: *"You're MEAN!"*

Me: *** CHALLENGE accepted***

Note for his son read:

I sleep too much, Parents complain.

I don't get enough sleep, Parents complain.

I eat too much, Parents complain.

I don't eat enough, Parents complain.

I am always in my room, Parents complain.

I go out too much, Parents complain.

I CAN'T WIN!

Next morning, he woke up a bit early and prepared their favorite breakfast. He sat at the breakfast table waiting for them. They both entered the dining room and sat down to have breakfast. Each of them started recollecting what they read and were giggling to themselves. Gaurav questioned his mom and she too did the same. They both shared what they read on the Notes. All of them had a hearty laugh and enjoyed their favorite breakfast together.

Humor

According to me, anything and everything in this world require a touch of humor. We enjoy movies, which have good humor in it. We enjoy the company of friends and family members who add that tinge of humor in the gatherings. So, why restrict it only to that. Bringing humor in your day-to-day life will not only distress you but also your Teenager. Make sure to watch some funny movies together with them. It is the best stress buster for any Teenager. Do not lose an opportunity of cracking jokes. Laugh loud, laugh often and for a long time and see how this spreads across. Most of the time, only one of the parents has that humor in-built in their nature. Therefore, you can decide if you want to be the one or let your partner be the one. If both of you are the serious kind, then let someone else do the job for you. It could be your Teen's sibling, a cousin or a close relative with whom they connect well. This works wonder to make the negative atmosphere at home vanish.

Humor can relieve the stress of a negative situation or a moment. It could also turn the situation into a positive one and improve the bonding that you feel with your children. Laughter and humor heal your upset moods, calm down your anger and satisfy your role as a parent. Sometimes it gets difficult to break a moment of tension during a conflict. On the verge of anger, you might hurt either your self-esteem or the self-esteem of your Teenager. Most of the time, our cultural background, our brought up, our attitude and our nature decide how we react to a humorous situation. So, when you try to add some color to your life by either playing a funny prank or cracking a small joke, make sure you are aware of how the opposite person is going to react. You should not ridicule or pass any sarcastic comment to irritate or to provoke them. Be consciously aware and try to be sure of the different ways in which your Teenager might react to what you call the positive humor. Then use the right quantity of this tasty ingredient to your parenting pie recipe.

Add Your Creative Juices

Come on Friends, get started, and let your creative juices flow....

Have fun, add all the TOPPINGS you always enjoyed during your Teenage years or the ones that you always yearned for but never got, toppings which your Teen loves to have. "This is the time" ... Get Going....

Sharing a few toppings that my husband and I added on to our 'Parenting Pie', since my Teenage daughter enjoys the PIE more with these Toppings.

Ingredient for Topping	*Measure*
Cooking her favorite dish	Once in two weeks
Hugs and Kisses	More number of times than her brother (I know you might think I am mean, but I do it without offending my little one)
Window shopping with her in a Mall (Mom and Daughter time)	Once in 3 months
Family time watching a movie on Netflix	Once every month
Family vacation	Once in a year
Permission to spend time with her friends over a movie/lunch (I still instill the conditions for this, but yet she gets the permission if it does not disturb her schedules)	Whenever she gets an invitation

Ingredient for Topping	*Measure*
Celebrating Birthday with her friends	Milestone Birthdays
Purchasing her favorite novel	Whenever she requests for it and confirms, she will read it only during her break time. This helps in putting her off the screen time using her phone or iPad

Now that you know all the ingredients, you can come with your own methods of making and baking the PIE for your TEEN. Add a touch of your own parental style to it. As I told you earlier, without a parent's personal touch, the dish is incomplete. So, enjoy creating a customized recipe for your Teenager. Well, you can surely involve them in deciding the ingredients too. That will also help you understand, which one is more important for them and in what measure…..

Customized "Parenting Pie" Recipe for Your Teenager

Ingredients for Crust

Ingredient	Measure

Ingredient	Measure

Ingredients for the Filling

Ingredient	Measure

Ingredient	Measure

Ingredients for the Toppings

Ingredient	Measure

Ingredient	Measure

Method

Summary and
Best Wishes

A child is just a little seedling with tiny leaves above the earth, peeping out into the air for the first time. It is very easy for that seedling to get crushed into the ground by harsh words, or making judgements. This leaves the tiny shoot bruised, battered and unable to rise again. You have to care for it, protect and nurture it until it becomes stronger. Then when the wind and rain hit it hard, it will learn to bend but will not be crushed. It will even become stronger as it resists the push of the weather, but still, it will be vulnerable. You need to care for your Teenager as you would for any fragile new life.

Our children are our gift to the future. What they experience at our homes today will empower them to bring to the world they inherit, the ways that affirm the dignity and humanity of all the people.

Thank you for joining me in this journey through my mindset. You must be heaving a sigh of relief after understanding that you are not alone. Now that you are more equipped with handling the situations that happen at home every day, do make an effort to practice bits and pieces of the Parenting recipe until you master it with your Teenagers.

If you have found this book useful, I would really appreciate a review or a share on social media. It would really help more people to discover the book and also get the required help.

Share with me your stories and incidents of learning from your Teens at the below survey:

Life Lessons Learnt from Your Teenagers

Want to learn more about how to become a great parent with whom your Teenager can communicate like a friend but follow your instructions like a parent? Get your Teenage Parent Blueprint created by me and watch the video series at:

www.praveensinghmuni.com/parentingpie

Join my Facebook Page

http://www.facebook.com/ParentingPie

to discuss, share and get to know what's happening in the lives of other Parents.

"BE READY TO TRANSFORM YOURSELF AND YOUR AWESOME TEENAGERS."

Good Luck….

—Praveen Singh

www.ingramcontent.com/pod-product-compliance
Lightning Source LLC
LaVergne TN
LVHW091458170726
843492LV00001B/236